Loss of Voice

Loss of Voice

My Poetic Journey

Dr. Chris M. McDaniel

iUniverse, Inc.
New York Lincoln Shanghai

Loss of Voice
My Poetic Journey

Copyright © 2006 by Dr. Chris M. McDaniel

All rights reserved. No part of this book may be used or reproduced by any means, graphic, electronic, or mechanical, including photocopying, recording, taping or by any information storage retrieval system without the written permission of the publisher except in the case of brief quotations embodied in critical articles and reviews.

iUniverse books may be ordered through booksellers or by contacting:

iUniverse
2021 Pine Lake Road, Suite 100
Lincoln, NE 68512
www.iuniverse.com
1-800-Authors (1-800-288-4677)

ISBN-13: 978-0-595-39854-6 (pbk)
ISBN-13: 978-0-595-84253-7 (ebk)
ISBN-10: 0-595-39854-5 (pbk)
ISBN-10: 0-595-84253-4 (ebk)

Printed in the United States of America

For my parents:
Who gave me the gift of life,
and the lessons to live it.

Contents

For your reading pleasure, the poems have been listed alphabetically, rather than numerically, so you can easily find certain poems you may be looking for.

18-C	18
A BATTLE LOST	105
A CHANCE	3
A DECEMBER TO REMEMBER	111
A HELPING HAND	46
A LESSON TO LEARN	113
A MYSTIC NIGHT	142
A PIRATE STORY	27
A STORM IN MY MIND	36
ABOVE	108
ABSENCE	95
ALEXANDER & SON, INC.	53
ANGEL	44
AS I REMEMBER GRANDMA	63
ASTRONOMICAL EFFORTS	80
BEEZIE	89
BETRAYED BY THE OTHER	122
BLINDING	64
BOOMERANG	125

BUILT TO LAST?	65
CAREGIVER	117
CAVE CITY FIVE-O	102
CHORUS OF CONFUSION	34
CHURCH OF TOMMOROW	51
CLASSROOM SURRENDER	119
DARKNESS	54
DESERVE	10
DID I?	149
DISCOVER CHIROPRACTIC	67
DISORDER	9
DON'T PINCH ME NOW	11
ENDANGERED	112
ESCAPE	28
EVERASTING BLISS	21
EXTINCTION	68
FANTASTIC AT FIFTY	69
FASHIONABLY FIFTY	58
FIREPLACE PHILOSOPHY	73
FLAT TIRE	70
FOREVER AND ALWAYS	98
FUTURE DREAMS	19
GO BIG BLUE	97
GOODBYE	129
GRATITUDE	128
HELL'S FIRE	30

HERE COMES THE EAGLE	79
HOPELESS	121
I PRAY	24
ILLEGAL MEANS ILLEGAL	40
IN FRONT OF YOU	23
INSANITY	39
IT	26
IT IS MINE	118
KEY TO HAPPINESS	103
LAS TORTUGAS	42
LAST TRIAL	75
LIES	49
LIFE 101	57
LIFE'S BLOOD	115
LILIAN	87
LION AWAKES AGAIN	17
LOSS OF VOICE	1
LOST	62
LOST, BUT NOT FORGOTTEN	16
LOVE	61
MATH 113	90
MOTHER CHRISTMAS	82
MY CAPTAIN	2
MY CHAIR	55
MY FATHER, MY FRIEND	7
MY SISTER'S GLOW	76

MYSTIC KNIGHTS OF THE OINGO BOINGO	107
NOT THE ONE	104
ON MY MIND	59
ONE ENCHANTED EVENING	109
ONE VOICE	25
OPEN	140
OUR WORLD	114
PARROTHEADS	126
PERFECT LIFE	85
POP SMARTS	6
POWDER KING	83
PRECIOUS PERFECT	47
PREJUDICIAL NONSENSE	5
RAISE YOUR HANDS	144
RECONCILIATION	41
REPUTATION	37
RESOLUTION	35
SEEDS TO GROW	94
SHATTERED	38
SILVER ANNIVERSARY	91
STRAWBERY PRESERVES	43
SURVIVAL	99
THANKS FOR THE MEMORIES	77
THE DREAMER'S RUN	4
THE END	131
THE ETERNAL JOURNEY	12

THE GIRL	143
THE GOOD LIFE	136
THE GREAT FLOOD	84
THE LIGHTHOUSE	45
THE LOCKER	127
THE MAZE OF LIFE	13
THE MOVING PICTURE SHOW	123
THE TIMES	71
THESE VOWS	15
THIS WORLD BELOW	93
TODAY AND TOMORROW	20
TODAY, I AM A CHIROPRACTOR	101
TRAVELIN' MAN	33
TREES	48
TRUE REFLECTIONS	29
UNDYING PASSION	74
WALK THE LINE	66
WEDDED BLISS	56
WHO'S THIS GIRL?	88
WITHHELD	31
WITHOUT	120
YES I & I	81
YOU TOLD ME	138

Introduction

As I revise my body of work for publication, I am amazed at the emotions that these words can still evoke within me. You will find that I am touched by many things, and in turn, put paper to pen to express my innermost feelings. My wonderful family, my amazing friends, my favorite music, and my passions for travel, endangered animals and the sea, are a common thread in this collection that spans the better part of my life.

I wrote my first poem on a flight to Hawaii when I was nine years old, and haven't stopped yet. I have been blessed with so many things throughout my life, that I simply had to send these "lyrical moments" to print. So many of the poems are of a personal nature, yet I believe that if you understand my zest for adventure, and my passion for warmth and togetherness, that you will feel the impact of the poems, as they were intended when I first wrote them.

Loss of Voice represents the culmination of numerous events in my life, and I hope that you will enjoy following my poetic journey through this amazing roller coaster ride. I am sharing my most private views on racism, terrorism, hatred, crime, death, and extinction; yet try to balance the book with a majority of romance, birthdays, weddings, humor, celebrations, prayers, songs and optimism.

This manuscript has had many names, held many forms, and was rejected by several different publishers before this last submission. I have scribbled poems on napkins in some of the nicest restaurants in the world, on some of the bumpiest plane rides, and on brochures in some of the nation's dingiest motels. I have written poems for pleasure, and I have written poems in pain. Through my years of education, relationships, employment and travel, I have always turned to poetry, and assume I always will. Poetry is my voice, when no one else is listening.

Life is my muse, and rhyme is my gift to you.

Enjoy and God bless.

Dr. Chris M. McDaniel

LOSS OF VOICE

Island clothes and Buffett shows
The palm trees, sea, and sand
My journey's just beginning
But my life's turned out like planned

When I set sail two decades back
To start my education
I never knew I'd be so blessed
To find my true vocation

Established private practice
After all my schooling ended
Got settled in my house
But lost the voice I'd once befriended

This voice I'd lost was poetry
Expression, time forgot
I had the bills and workload
But I had the free time not

So now that I've got time to spare
Life's firmly on its track
I've put my pen to paper
Since I got my lost voice back

I welcome you to read these words
And share my private feelings
I've gathered twenty years of rhyme
To share with you my dealings

From family travels, books and song
To years of earthly pleasures
My poems speak of dreams and schemes
That led to heartfelt treasures

Enjoy these next few pages
Where I came from, where I've been
I hope when 'Volume Two' gets done
Our paths will cross again.

MY CAPTAIN

I've sailed this sea a thousand times
I've dropped my anchor deep

I often put the sails up high
And drift while I'm asleep

To islands lost, yet full of life
I make my ports of call

The treasures there, unlimited
Shall build my stature tall

The sun, the sand and crystal waters
Share one common purpose

To aide a dreamer's dreaming
While behind his dream he searches

A paradise surrounds me
My reality unnoticed

I board my vessel once again
Uncharted land, my focus

Crashing wave's gigantic swells
The hull goes smashing through

This water separates me
From the world I know so true

A world that's full of horror
Full of pain, and my mistakes

A world that I must conquer
When my captain here awakes.

A CHANCE

Their blood runs through their veins like ours
They differ from each other

They all give birth to thriving young
To be nursed by their mother

They live and die, like mortal men
As murder sweeps the land

A poacher strives to take the lives
That he won't understand

Creatures here since our creation
Walked upon this earth

When man decides to claim this prize
He wastes a sacred birth

Their hooves, their horns, their hides, their hearts
Belong to mankind not

For man will wipe existence clean
Those species life forgot

So men upon this earth I beg
Improve endangered stance

Allow to breathe, to live, to fly
For all deserve the chance.

THE DREAMER'S RUN

Atop the world in silence
As I've conquered my last goal

From body came my spirit
And my heart released my soul

Eternal signs of travel
Now appear to guide the way

Starting on my journey
To the never ending day

Where rain won't fall and wind won't blow
Where all can live as one

Where wishes from a far off star
Can halt the dreamer's run

Your dreams become reality
Those wishes do get granted

This land of treasure lies within
Yet still remains enchanted

You need not journey far to reap
The harvest of this love

Just close your eyes and hold your heart
For all will rise above.

PREJUDICIAL NONSENSE

Stereotypical evidence
Cannot prove true to me

Discrimination's stupor
Still distorts the way we see

Skin of different color
Different sex, and different mind

Each one of us are brothers
For our race is humankind

America, our heritage
Her skin is tough and strong

A rainbow of democracy
Shall end a nightmare long

So join me in my quest for peace
May racist viewpoints change

God's children will unite this earth
And halt these hateful ways.

POP SMARTS

Hidden in my little box
Inside my thin foil wrapper

I live here in this cupboard
With the bread, the chips, and crackers

The sun goes down, to rise again
Its breakfast time once more

We almost start to cry
When hungry people hit that door

I dread that kid's decision
Is it I, or toast & jelly

He glances at the toaster
Rubs his hand atop his belly

We rearrange within our box
"Oh maybe he won't pick me!"

The eight of us start praying
That he might just have rice crispies

He reaches up to grab for me
Now off into the toaster

He drops me in, then sits back with
His orange juice on its coaster

I slowly start to melt inside
My heat is sure to learn him

And hopefully to teach him good
My frosting's going to burn him.

MY FATHER, MY FRIEND

From shooting hoops in our backyard
To climbing in that tree

Through twenty years of my short life
My dad's been there for me

From driving through the Nation's Parks
And touring this great land

My father takes good care of me
My daddy understands

He knows me like a well-read book
He knows my every move

I've learned this all the hard way
But I once thought I was smooth

His love of UK basketball
Once led to where I learned

His love of caves and caverns
Once led me to where I earned

I value his opinion wise
And give him my respect

He does for me such giving things
At times I don't expect

So thank you dad, for teaching me
The rights and wrongs of way

I hope you know I cherish you
And love you, everyday.

While studying abnormal psychology at the University of Kentucky, I wrote several poems for the lost souls who wandered the halls of the saddening, maddening mental wards.

Disorder, Hopeless, It is Mine, Escape, Chorus of Confusion, Resolution, Hell's Fire and *Insanity* are just a few of the poems written during those years.

I hope that our awareness of mental illness and chemical imbalance continues to grow, because these individuals are truly ill, and need our care and concern. They are in a desperate situation that they don't deserve.

We need to give them the hope that they need, to believe that their conditions can improve.

DISORDER

Terror of abandonment
Has often left me stranded

Dysmorphic thoughts of reason
Seem to leave me empty handed

Hollowed by refraction
From the battles that we've fought

Renaissance in action
For no teaching need be taught

Borderline hysteria
Still often clouds my mind

Preventing joy and sanity
Emotions I can't find

The sun won't shine on me today
Below this raining shower

Lost in constant sorrow
From this dreadful reigning power

I only hope tomorrow halts
And doesn't come to haunt me

For each day brings a new surprise
Of evil that will taunt me.

DESERVE

You don't deserve the love I give
You don't deserve my touch

You don't deserve the words I say
With love I feel so much

You don't deserve the songs I sing
Or all the lines I write

You don't deserve the warmth you get
All hours of the night

And all the things I've given you
To you they don't belong

For, once I thought you did deserve
But now I see, I'm wrong.

DON'T PINCH ME NOW

I think that I should share with you, just how I'm feeling now
And if you feel the same for me, we'll make it through somehow

You don't come with instructions, and you're not like all the rest
Love under construction, and I've hired just the best

These past few weeks, I can't explain the way emotion's grown
There's nothing here I think is great, its something that I know

Your hair, no matter how it's worn, is perfect on your head
Your words no matter how they come, are perfect when they're said

Your eyes can light the darkest depths of dismal caves below
Your smile is brighter than the hue of newly fallen snow

A protein here, a carb no less, a veggie, don't forget
Your mannerisms make me smile, they don't make me upset

For in the future I can't see, a solitary fight
No battles over stupid things, no wars throughout the night

So thank you dearest beauty for the smile upon my face
And know that you are welcome here, forever in this place

I truly feel I'm dreaming, and I hope I sleep forever
For if this treasure is a dream, don't pinch me now, not ever.

THE ETERNAL JOURNEY

Ablaze in the sky was a fiery wind
When I suddenly felt a cool breeze on my skin

With nothing to lose and with all hope to gain
I closed both my eyes and I felt no restrain

Before I had noticed, my feet had left ground
Except for my breath, I could not hear a sound

I clinched my fists tight and I opened my eyes
With no earth below me, I felt no surprise

I knew that all good things soon come to an end
So I treasured the times that may not come again

As I marveled the visions that stood in my sight
I continued to soar with no boundaries that night

I sailed through the distance without looking back
And I kept mind in focus without losing track

I felt a warm feeling of love in my heart
For the earthly creations that soon I would part

The oceans, the valleys, the rivers, and plains
The joys and the laughter, the sorrows and pains

My infinite voyage had taken no time
And a life without reason was now filled with rhyme.

THE MAZE OF LIFE

A basketball into its hoop
The earth goes down the drain

It seems that hearts have been replaced
By evil, hateful brains

The quality has lost control
The quantity is spreading

While cardboard's used for house's walls
And concrete's used for bedding

Thieves that steal can reproduce
And little thieves they'll raise

A couple with respect and love
Will send kids through this maze

Our world is shot, it's our demise
But did we ask for terror?

Let filth and crime go answer that
While they look in the mirror

Our only hope is out of reach
This life already lives

We must evolve to teach the takers
They must learn to give.

As you will see throughout this collection, I have written poems for world events, and events that have meant the world to some people. Some of the happiest days of my life are captured in verse, and also some of the saddest. I have written poems for loved one's funerals (*Lost, But Not Forgotten,* and *Beezie*), I have written poems for birthdays, and I have written poems for weddings.

These Vows, was the first of many wedding poems, and holds a special place in my heart because, not only was it my first, it was written for a close friend.

I only preface this poem, because I believe that all of my personal poems will mean more to you, if you understand that they were all written for special people in my life, and that the emotions in all of my poetry are real, and they are my own.

THESE VOWS

A heart so full of kindness
Has met one in the same

And as this couple takes these vows
They state them in God's name

That through the coldest winter
And in those hardest times

They'll stand beside each other
As these wedding bells do chime

And when the sun is shining
When the clouds don't fill the sky

Their love will grow in time
With every day that passes by

A love we know has flourished
It's a love that's meant to be

Togetherness so strong and true
That anyone could see

So in the eyes of many
As they make this final stand

A man vows to a woman
With this ring upon her hand

That in this life of marriage
Through the best of their endeavors

Their hearts will hold each other dear
They vow this now, forever.

LOST, BUT NOT FORGOTTEN

A loss can make you realize
What having someone meant

Or make you recollect the past
And how your time was spent

A caring uncle, your best friend
A loving, special person

The sudden theft of your control
Can make your sorrow worsen

But time can take that pain away
To heal a saddened wound

In joyful, loving memories
Your pain will be consumed

The gloom shall turn to happiness
The present turns to past

Where love and admiration
Build a spirit that will last

Let's not forget the love they shared
When lives on earth were crossed

For now our Father watches over
Those that we have lost.

We miss you Uncle Woody.

LION AWAKES AGAIN

Robert Nesta Marley
Born in 1945

The power of this man
Not in another man alive

Belief and understanding
Of the world and all around us

Love and admiration
For the times he said had found us

Striving to share peace and joy
With every step he took

A thriving need to live his life
According to The Book

A way of life unorthodox
Was shown with locks in dread

A way to get his point across
With every word he said

Generations past and present
Feed upon his song

The future lives so touched by him
Shall prove his cause so strong

For only one love shall exist
One evil may not bother

See in the end, with truth exposed
We all come from one Father.

18-C

From hundreds of empty spaces
I have chosen one for me
I strap myself into my spot
It's labeled 18-C

There's two more here on my side
And there's three there on my right
A small foot-wide escarpment
Separates us during flight

We may all be just strangers
And enough into our years
To understand, the other hand
We all share common fears

"Did he do all those flap things right?"
"He knows what's in his hands?"
"Is he sure to put the big wheels down,
When he proceeds to land?"

So I'll rest in my 'piece'
Of this plane, called 18-C
Where a tiny exit door it seems
Is all that would save me

A simple common error
From the air down to the land
We'd all be trapped here in our seats
I just can't understand

Oh why I fret and worry
Every time I board this bird
When the voice of my confusion
Is a voice that can't be heard

These thoughts will someday falter
And they'll stay right here within
Until of course my boarding call's
What they'll be calling then.

FUTURE DREAMS

Time and time again
I get the pass but drop the ball

My body tells me something
But my mind can't hear the call

I strive to do my best in life
I work to stay on top

I want to topple all my goals
Before my heartbeats stop

On sunny days, or clouded skies
My efforts won't be faltered

My thoughts and feelings speak to me
My dreams will not be altered

For what I want will come to me
I won't give up the fight

And things I want, but don't need yet
Will fill my dreams tonight.

TODAY AND TOMORROW

This is the day the lord hath made
With you as the engineer

To fulfill your dreams and work your schemes
To bring the distant near

With goals in sight, and heart-held fright
Do not lose hope 'til you're through

With so many choices and unanswered voices
Your whole life's been left up to you

The day you were born, before clothes were worn
You were instantly put in control

With so much to say, and things in your way
Destruction will not hurt your soul

Excuse evolution and help the solution
Earth's destiny lies in your hands

Now that you've met me, please don't forget me
Let's make all the world understand.

EVERASTING BLISS

A door of utter happiness has opened unto me
And blindness from the love I feel, restrains the things I see

I think I see forever, yet the vision isn't pure
The fog lifts and it's clearer now, forever's there for sure

I see my perfect beauty, hair of gold and eyes of blue
I see my future lady, and I see my children too

I see a heart to guide and keep me, warm throughout the night
I feel the warm embrace of one, whose soul will hold me tight

I hear a silent whisper as the wind blows through the trees
I strain to see the goddess who has brought me to my knees

I feel the heat of passion when she lay within my arms
I taste the tears of pleasure, for I'll keep her safe from harm

I understand the riddle of my life without my queen
I know that here without her, my life's slate would be wiped clean

I shower her with goodness from the strength I gain above
And from this mighty power I am bathed within her love

I send to her sweet nothings, and I say to her these rhymes
My angel here will carry me, when lost within the times

I see the perfect wedding dress, the cake, the rice, balloons
And by my special someone, there I stand, I'm now the groom

I cannot tell this space in time, or if it's far from near
I see our friends and family, all their smiles and all their tears

My sweet and gorgeous beauty, now as sure as life is grand
I want to prove this love to you, so please now take my hand

And tell me that you'll leave me not, and love me like you've never
So vow to me you'll hold me, as you grasp me now, forever.

This was the poem written for my little sister's wedding, where my Uncle Don, who beautifully performed the ceremony, asked me to read the poem to the church.

I hate reading my own work, but reluctantly I accepted. Too bad I can't include the DVD with the book, because a blubbering big brother might really help sell this to the sensitive crowd.

In tears, I barely made it through the poem, but it was a special time, and I hope that everyone can have a wedding as beautiful as theirs was.

IN FRONT OF YOU

So hard to put to paper, all the words I cannot say
To share my joy with all of you who've gathered here today

In front of you, all dressed in white, my oldest, dearest friend
We think, and talk, and act the same, she's practically my twin

And next to her all dressed in black, a statue on a shelf
Couldn't have picked a better man if I'd done so myself

She's sweet and caring, kind and sharing, the groom found such a catch
His warmth and generosity, make them an ideal match

My Uncle Don stands proud and tall, to join these two in life
Our Keri's found the perfect man; Matt's found his perfect wife

So mom cries tears of joy today, and daddy, well, just cries
The beauty of this day will bring us happiness and smiles

To close, I wish the best of luck, to the bride and to the groom
I'd also like to recognize the miracle in this room

When I was only two I got a sister like no other
Today God blesses me again, as he gives me a brother.

Congratulations Matthew and Keri

June 22, 2002

I PRAY
My prayer for victims of the Oklahoma City bombing

Words cannot express the loss, so felt throughout this nation
A senseless act of violence, no cause nor explanation

The lives we've lost, we won't forget, their memories now are priceless
Hopes of certain justice leave a trail that shall entice us

I must convey my sadness, for the families and their friends
I hope you will accept from me, the love in which I send

I pray for you that strength in will, shall bring a peace to mind
I pray that God will help you understand our world's unkind

And maybe time will soon provide a reason for this pain
And time will one day shine joy's sun, where clouds of doom now reign

I pray for truth, for those we've lost, are in a better place
Where terrorists no longer harm, away from earth's disgrace

I pray for work and rescue crews, for fast and endless effort
May all the thanks that they deserve, continue now, forever

I pray for those they've left behind, the children kept from safety
I pray for mothers, fathers and the helpless crying babies.

God be with those in pain. Amen.

ONE VOICE

Oblivious to reasoning
The riots ramble on

Martin Luther, Malcolm X
The peace they sought is gone

There is no sense of unity
There's no one left to blame

We're burdened by confusion
And we're losers to this game

But every opposition, to oppression
Stands a chance

Let not the trials of history
Decide our future's stance

Believe within each other
For one race will rule the land

Not white, nor black, nor red, nor brown
Will hold the upper hand

The one race that I speak of
Is the race of humankind

One love, one earth, one future
For one's heart shall rule one's mind.

IT

Unstoppable in magnitude
Its violence steadily rose

Its outlook on destruction
Uncontrollably still grows

With no regard for human life
No prejudice, nor choice

It spreads across the planet
With a scarred and deadly voice

To speak its mind on chaos
And expressing all its thought

It wins without combatants
For no battle need be fought

It answers yet to no one
For it has no higher source

It simply raids the peacefulness
And stays upon its course

With no hope to control the beast
We must just let it be

And understand the awful IT
May lie there, within thee.

A PIRATE STORY

Three ships sail the seven seas
With treasure in their sights

Landing in those tropic waters
Proving strength through fights

From islands near to islands far
They scavenge and they search

For diamonds, emeralds, rubies
And the gold of purest worth

From fear of Blackbeard's temper
And a fear of Captain Cook

We even fear the make believe
Like those with shiny hooks

On wooden legs, with sword at side
An eye patch on their brow

The skills of thieving aimlessly
Lay hidden in their scowl

May not the likes of pirates old
Corrupt the sailors mind

May not the quest for pirate's gold
Deter your treasure's find.

ESCAPE

Alone in walls of anguish
Still I cannot leave this tomb

From my despair and sadness
My depression fills this room

A door swings out in front of me
I turn to walk that way

It closes and reminds me then
Of things I didn't say

This door is my confusion
As I choose from right and wrong

My list of proper choices now
Is far from reaching long

I've made mistakes and paid the price
And now see what I've done

I've fought the battle, lost the war
And darkness has been won

So as I lay in silence here
Between redemption's walls

I pray that soon I may escape
To walk exemption's halls.

TRUE REFLECTIONS

Expressions from my inner soul
Have led me to this place

A mirror of reality
Reflects to me, my face

But not the face I've always known
That's not the face I see

Resemblance quite revealing
But the glass does not show me

I view a mind of quality
Where content isn't there

A mind full of confusion
But where memory seems quite bare

With past and present far between
No further zeal for life

To comprehend my visions near
I must appeal my strife

With onward stride to start anew
I feed on this expression

I'll focus on this changing view
To see my true reflection.

HELL'S FIRE

From graves of bones and shadows
And from victim's lonely cries

The ghosts and goblins everywhere
Begin to slowly rise

To fill the void with silence
And to keep your fear inside

When ghouls and monsters come to town
There's nowhere you can hide

And though we must control them child
We must still stand our ground

To keep the demons out of sight
Before we hear no sound

For, once they get beneath your skin
Not one thing can you do

The madmen in the streets
Can only hope they'll get to you

And venture to the dark side
From where no one can return

From heaven's earthly pleasures
To the fires of hell you'll burn.

WITHHELD

Exemption from democracy
Has led to where I stand
Decision is the only force
That I feel close at hand

I can't express my proper feelings
Cannot speak my mind
I now engage in common fears
So shared by all mankind

Only to expose my thoughts
And set emotion free
I feel I must contain myself
And not confide in thee

I know that true confessions
Will resolve my inner strife
Explaining that these actions rare
Epitomize my life.

I speak many times throughout this book about the impact that family has had on my life. My great grandfather, an orator named Dr. Elwood Rowsey was a 33rd degree Mason (the highest honor the fraternity can bestow). Both of my grandfathers were also members of the worlds oldest fraternity; Martie Vernon McDaniel was made a Master Mason in Park City, Kentucky, and Rev. Bill Alexander was a 32nd degree Scottish Rite Mason in Oklahoma City, Oklahoma.

Unfortunately, I never met any of these great men. For this reason, I decided to join this storied organization, to follow in the same footsteps that all those men before me had to walk, getting me a little bit closer to the men I never knew.

I am a currently a 32nd degree Mason, a Perpetual Life member of Scottsdale Lodge #43, and a Life Endowed member of the Phoenix Scottish Rite Bodies.

I truly believe that this fraternity, rich with tradition, constantly does amazing things for our society, and plays an immeasurable role in globally assisting humanity.

TRAVELIN' MAN

A Mason's job is never through
A brother's role, unending
A lifelong bond that ties us to
Tradition's hold, unbending

I walked within the footsteps
Of a greater man than I
To sit in lodge with Brethren dear
Beneath a starry sky

A handshake and a smile
Make my intentions known to others
A helping nature, warm with grace
Let's me know they're my brothers

A square and compass guide me
Through the land a King once ruled
A level keeps me grounded
As I use their working tools

Washington and Franklin
Founded land of peace and glory
Establishing a liberty
To tell Freemason's stories

The secrets in the rumor mill
Won't do us any harm
The truth lies in our history
With virtue, truth and charm

Despite tradition's past
Our lives are still misunderstood
Our legacy was built to last
God bless this Brotherhood.

CHORUS OF CONFUSION

Aristocratic evidence
To Hippocratic oath

I must refuse conformity
And disregard them both

A pathway of uncertainty
Lay deep beneath my feet

The choices and decisions
In my life, remain discreet

Allowing me with slow progression
Living day by day

To reach the goals my dreams have led
I go my separate way

Avoiding both the voice of reason
And my inner soul

The footsteps of my destiny
Are stomping my life's goals

A chorus of confusion heard aloud
Throughout my mind

Is turning wheels of torture
While the gears of joy unwind

Abrasions from my suffering
Along with sorrow's woes

Will help me find solution's path
And follow where it goes.

RESOLUTION

R is for the mere respect in which I do now seek

E is for emotion that shall keep the wicked meek

S is for the suffering that ails my heart and soul

O is for the age of guilt, my problems do grow old

L is for the love in mind when pleasant thoughts arise

U is for undying strength, I'll not withhold my cries

T is for my testimony, bold, and full of truth

I is for my instincts, for they keep my thoughts aloof

O is for, it's over, for I'll find the end somehow

N is for my senses, may they please come to me now.

A STORM IN MY MIND

Clouds of indecision fill my mind as time goes by
Indifference to equality has made these rain clouds dry

Expulsion of a precious heart, done wrong by glacier's ice
Has fallen into my care now, my sunshine must suffice

I must now free my senses, to emancipate my soul
To lend a hand in times of need is now my only goal

Withheld inside like flurries, feelings hard to understand
For when my problems surface, a solution lay at hand

The stress and tension bury me, as now I gasp for air
And underneath my own demise, I've only had one care

To share the thoughts inside my head, before my storm begins
For when the clouds roll in tonight, the pain will fall again.

REPUTATION

A dive to mediocrity
Has put you in your place

A lack of popularity
Now stares you in the face

Your friends have turned their backs on you
You've lost your sense of pride

A stagger in your step
Now proves a swagger in your stride

Mistakes are stacked against you
Odds no longer have control

You've got no hope, you can't turn back
No ace is in the hole

Giving up will lead to nowhere
Simply your destruction

The way you built your image up
Was based on poor construction

An obstacle at every turn
Will bring your ruin faster

I hope your shattered ego's wounds
Will save you from disaster.

SHATTERED

Standards falling, hunger's calling
Will the madness stop?

Raising prices, greed entices
Farmers lose their crop

People walking aimlessly
In homeless states of mind

Emptied hearts and buried spirits
Make their world unkind

Without the mere compassion
That a human soul deserves

Unseen by our society
Their vision here is blurred

Afraid to simply walk the streets
Afraid to stand alone

Ashamed to see the truth revealed
A fear your eyes have shown

A storm of lifeless feeling
Now encompasses our land

A cold, uncaring tempest
Will tempt warmth to take a stand.

INSANITY

Along the lines of sanity
A thin line comes between
A thought possessed by demons
Is the only thought you've seen

A mind with bad intention
And a soul from evil's core
Has led you to this sacred place
And you don't know what for

An overview of common sense
With no regard for logic
Has started to unravel
With in mind, no hopes to stop it

For only if you delve within
The reaches of your self
Shall all the books of horror
Get placed back upon the shelf

And one day soon your sun will rise
To wake your dismal life
Then, and only then you'll find
A freedom from your strife

ILLEGAL MEANS ILLEGAL

I've got to get a few words down
On U.S. Immigration
Our border's not invisible
There's been no invitation

In my opinion, immigrants
Have made us what we are
But that all happened legally
They worked to get their cards

I can't believe how often now
I hear the dreaded stories
Of increased problems in our land
Erasing all our glory

The founding fathers did their job
To form a better nation
They even made provisions for
This beast called immigration

Learn the language, pay your taxes
Then you shall be welcomed
It simply has to be that way
When legal, I say "Help 'Em!"

Help them get a driver's license
Help them get a job
Help them live a life like mine
Let not their families sob

My heart is open unto you
My country can be too
Just go about it legally
Then all would welcome you

Just do the things I'd have to do
Then that will make it fair
Treat us just like we'd treat you
America...we'll share.

RECONCILIATION

Diligent to seek redemption
Adamant to try

Enforcing laws from inner truth
As time still passes by

Expulsion from society
Has made the tension strong

A healing road less traveled
Will expand the journey long

Freedom from your horrid past
Will find you making well

The demons of your consciousness
That told you time would tell

Consumed within your own demise
You wallow in the pain

Sadness caused by your own lies
Which trust constructs in vain.

LAS TORTUGAS

Islands of the sacred turtle
Cayman's past be known

Destination paradise
The Cayman's stand alone

Beaches of the purest sand
As white as winter's snow

Where palm tree shade is cool like ice
Wherever feet may roam

An underwater majesty
A diver's truest love

To breathe and swim in water's deep
Forgetting worlds above

Enchanting walls of coral
Living reef from ocean's dead

A picture tells a thousand words
When not one word be said

Mystic colors, aqua greens
The reds and azure blues

Beneath the water lies a world
Discovered by so few

Protect the Cayman Islands
Please don't make me fight alone

Preserve the turtle's livelihood
Our playground is their home.

STRAWBERY PRESERVES

Trapped inside my small glass cage
Beneath a lid of tin

I can't escape this Mason's jar
I'm trapped here, stuck within

I'm sticking to myself in here
I'm cramped and squished inside

So jammed within my single cell
In you, I now confide

I'd like to live a life like yours
I'd like to have the choice

I'd love the chance to breathe fresh air
And speak my unheard voice

I guess this is my purpose
And my job to do in life

To hide away 'til one fine day
Uncovered by one's wife

Brought in from the storage shed
Or taken from the shelf

My cage is opened, I escape
To share with you, myself

I'm spread on top of many things
In many different places

So in the end, it's not so bad
For I bring smiles to faces.

ANGEL

Many years behind you,
We must count to be exact
An order came for beauty
And the heavens had to act

They went to work on something
Someone special, warm and true
God began his masterpiece
He started making you!

A mind that's sharp and brilliant
With a heart that can't be stopped
Eyes of endless color
In a gaze that can't be topped

Perfection in its truest form
He sent you down to earth
To bless a human family
With a blessed baby's birth

An angel sent from heaven
Like a star from outer space
I pray you keep that gorgeous smile
Upon your perfect face

And all year long remember
Just two things from me to you
We love the world you've made here,
And you know we love you too.

THE LIGHTHOUSE

The lighthouse old and lonely
Sets ablaze the moonlit sky

As sailors from the oceans
Set adrift from far and wide

As crashing foam explodes upon
The beach, the rocks and sand

The lighthouse lends the swaying ships
A timely, needed hand

Centuries of helping those
Who ride upon the waves

The mighty lighthouse stretches out
The old blind captain's cane

Reaching upward, top aglow
The lighthouse tried and true

Will guide you safe to harbor
When the sky has lost sun's hue.

A HELPING HAND

Can we ever work them out?
The trials of our past

The wars and riots, all that pain
Has left a scar to last

Bloodshed, un-fed, rapes and murders
Children lost to famine

Men and women lose their homes
Their kids become abandoned

But more and more each day, by day
The past becomes our future

An operation must be done
To mend us with love's suture

We must decide, when we arise
To change a life we meet

To laugh, to smile, to share your praise
To battle their defeat

Let's leave behind the world's contempt
Please help me make a stand

For all mankind to seek redemption
Won't you lend a hand?

PRECIOUS PERFECT

I feel a certain urgency
To spill my thoughts and feelings

The girl I miss has got to be
The reason my heart's reeling

I dream awake of her sweet love
Her smile and eyes like fire

I pray my dreaming never stops
And that her love won't tire

I see my baby everywhere
I'm sure she sees me too

Reminding me of kindness
There are visions here of you

I find my mind escapes me
And I can't complete my thoughts

My love for my sweet angel
Takes up all the love I've got

Her passion dominates my life
Perfection rules her world

And someday she will be my wife
My precious, perfect girl.

TREES

Branches growing outward
As they branch into the sky

Stretching, pulling, reaching up
They house the birds that fly

They give the world our true life's blood
The air in which we breathe

Homes and tools and paper too
More things than we'd conceived

It falls each year to quench their thirst
Forever, may it rain

Without respect for these great friends
Our planet shows no shame

So put away your chainsaws now
And find a better source

For lumber, cups and papers
Make recycling stay the course

Trees build us up, we cut them down
We must make up our minds

To leave the trees within the ground
Would better all mankind.

LIES

What a tangled web we weave
When others trust your word

To think we mean the things we say
Is really quite absurd

People do such sordid things
So different, night and day

Say what you mean, wipe this slate clean
Could you mean what you say?

Lies in time, can change your mind
Your focus can get lost

The truth revealed, is clearly named
The muse that bears your cross.

My grandfather, Rev. Bill Alexander was a pioneering man of God, and a legend in his own time. He was the preacher who married The King of The Cowboys, Roy Rogers to his wife and silver screen companion, Dale Evans. If you watch the Roy Roger's episode of "This Is Your Life," you will see him as the celebrity bait that brings Roy to the set; it really is fun to watch.

W.H. "Bill" Alexander also ran for a seat in the U.S. Senate (Oklahoma) in 1950. This was an amazing year in politics, as Richard Nixon was elected to the Senate before he later ran for the Presidency, and Prescott S. Bush (father of George H.W. Bush, grandfather of President George W. Bush) also, unsuccessfully ran for the U.S. Senate. All three were Republican candidates that year, only Nixon was victorious.

Dr. William H. Alexander single-handedly raised the money to build the First Christian Church, "Church of Tomorrow" in Oklahoma City, and was the pastor there for nearly twenty years before his untimely death in 1960. My uncle, Rev. Don H. Alexander later took the helm, and continued his father's mission for another 30 years.

Rev. Don Alexander is an amazingly wise father, husband, speaker, author (he has written several books), and friend. We are all lucky to have him in our lives. His wife, my Aunt Judy, and their children Ann Lynn and Eric are certainly treasured, and I hope that we will forever be close. Ann Lynn blessed them with Haley and Alex, and Eric is truly their shining Star.

My Uncle Don perpetuates the legacy that my grandfather began years ago, and with dignity, class and pride, he continues to share his many gifts with the world.

The following two poems were my gifts to him at his 25th anniversary, and his retirement from the church five years later.

CHURCH OF TOMMOROW

The words I place upon this page, are written from my heart
A truly giving man has given all I need to start

A reason to begin this poem and time to recognize
His many fine accomplishments, perfection's no surprise

Twenty-five impressive years, he's called this pulpit home
His warmth and giving nature, both his hearts and hands have shown

Ears to hear the poor lost souls, he guides them on their way
A voice to heal the worried, in his calm and peaceful way

A warm and helpful, gentle hand, outstretched to all he knows
His kindness is unequaled, as his faith in Jesus grows

He's true to his beliefs above; God's love has made him proud
For this, he stands each week to share, "the word" with this fine crowd

Through his successes many, and the ups and downs of life
He'll tell you that he's not alone, this thanks he owes his wife

Two children and their families also bless this happy clan
For this, the gift of happiness still gives to this great man

A blessed congregation, make his job a welcome trade
His goal to share the gospel, from the church his father made

Tradition, love, and happiness have built your joy from sorrow
Today we're blessed to have him, in this church built for tomorrow.

November 16, 1997

The first line of this poem was borrowed from one of my Grandfather's many fantastic sermons. I have used it several times in my work, in an attempt to emulate his greatness.

I am lucky that my Mother and my Uncles were able to share their wisdom with me through the years, and allow me to get a small glimpse of a man that I never knew.

While flying in a private plane to give the commencement address at Penn State University, a stormy crash took the lives of Bill and his wife Mary Louise. My mother was only eight years old when she lost her parents, and her undying strength is what has driven my family for as long as I can remember.

Someday a book will be written about Rev. W.H. Bill Alexander, and the world will know that we lost a wonderful man that night, He left a living legacy, and I'm proud to be a part of it.

ALEXANDER & SON, INC.

This is the day the Lord hath made, with you as the engineer
When all of your accomplishments were brought before us here

Atop this sacred stage, we've seen you walk within his shoes
In front of wide-eyed worshipers, words glued them to their pews

They've listen to the wisdom, forged through nearly fifty years
A father-and-son pulpit team, helped churn this church's gears

And from above, his eyes on you, his smile and bright red hair
How proud you make him standing there, as tears form in his stare

For without fail, you've done your all, to care for every soul
That walked into those stained glass halls, redemption was their goal

You helped the helpless, loved the hurt, shared smiles instead of sorrow
With God you kept your father's word, in *your* Church of Tomorrow.

September 15, 2002

DARKNESS

Everybody runs around, they're fleeing all about
And this is just what happens here, when all the lights go out

Darkness takes your vision, and your senses are impaired
If you are one who fears the night, you'll often become scared

I cannot, for the life of me, see why you need the light
Is it because of monsters, or of nightmare's ghostly fright

The nighttime's just like shadows, and yet they don't hurt your life
The darkness can be split in two, the sun's a sharpened knife

My words of wisdom, little friend, are "do not be afraid"
The demons cannot hurt you here, if all your dues are paid

But you must never tell a soul, about your weary fright
See this is how you pay those dues, to stay safe through the night

Secrets are the answer here, for, talking leads to pain
But keeping all those feelings in, could make one go insane

A mere two inches from your face, you cannot see your hand
It might be ground up bones you're on, and not the beach's sand

The moon is slowly setting, and the sun will soon come up
But don't go tell your frightening tales, you lost and helpless pup

And finally it's over now, you slowly see the sun
I know that you enjoyed it here, the dark is always fun.

MY CHAIR

I walked into my class today
And looked down at my seat

And as I viewed it up and down
I saw that it had feet

It got right up and left the room
Went straight into the hall

I chased it down and grabbed it
Then I threw it to the wall

It said to me, "You selfish thing,
Who do you think you are?

You ride me three days out of five,
For that, you've got a car!"

I said "I'm sorry, Mr. Chair,
I didn't know you hurt."

The chair replied, "Why can't you see
You treat me just like dirt!"

I felt about two inches tall
What pain I had implanted

All of this from selfishness
I took my chair for granted

I then began to walk away
I hung my head down low

I called back to my angry chair
"I'm sorry.... should've known."

WEDDED BLISS
For Tyler and Amie

A perfect love has found you
In a world of lost control

As two have joined together
Comes one life, one cherished soul

Hearts of warm compassion
Intertwine, like endless kissing

Together you will breathe as one
And lend the void what's missing

Side by side, through good and bad
You heal each other's pain

You smile and laugh together
In a bond with no restrain

And may your love protect you both
From sadness, pain and cold

For with these words I bless you
To remain unique and bold

I love you both so dearly,
And wish nothing but the finest

For all who know you, feel the warmth
That your love's put inside us.

LIFE 101

What's learned in class is soon forgotten
Wasted, useless knowledge

The teacher that you learn most from
Cannot be found in college

The chance to find your own true self
When freedom's gears get started

You might just find your own true love
You might get broken-hearted

A friend to last a lifetime long
Perhaps a future wife

A partner in your studies
Of the real world, now your life

What's learned in class is miniscule
Compared to social learning

May no one feed the ridicule
Identities start burning

Your homework calls for meeting those
To aide a lasting strife

Assignments that will guide you
With a passing grade in life.

FASHIONABLY FIFTY

I don't think that its possible, I know it can't be true
Fifty years on earth and not a bit of age on you

It seems like only yesterday, you lived at Diamond Caverns
You rebuilt from the ground up, decorations, plans, and patterns

And to the wild, wild west you went, when real estate was tamed
For no one out in Scottsdale could compete with our last name

And all the while you did this, working hard, day in, day out
You always found the time to show what life was all about

Vacations to the fifty states, and movies by the dozens
Trips to visit grandma, uncles, aunts and all our cousins

So as you helped to guide me, we picked Bluegrass for our home
Then sent me off to root Big Blue, my first time....all alone

But soon you all would follow, and to Bowling Green you'd fall
To find a home in State Farm, with Good Neighbors, one and all

Amazing, ageless mother, with no wrinkles on her face
Half a century filled your soul, with wisdom, love and grace

I've been around the world, to every ocean, land and sea
And nowhere is there such a perfect mom out there for me.

Happy Birthday Mom!

For mom's 50th Birthday party at the Bowling Green Country Club

March 19, 2002

ON MY MIND

This is just to share with you
You're always on my mind

I see you in the early morn
And in the moonlit sky

I feel you all around me
For I'm bare without your touch

I've not had such importance
Nothing's ever meant this much

Flowing through my every thought
My future and my past

An all surrounding, glowing love
Whose blindness here shall last

So this is just to let you know
You're always on my mind

From all the dreams in front of us
To memories far behind.

This poem was written for my family members that are peppered all over the world, our numerous family friends in Arizona and our neighbors on Sahuaro Drive, where I grew up in Scottsdale.

One couple in particular, Jerome and Marcelle Reiner, were two of our favorite neighbors, and trust me, we've had plenty. Sadly, I was recently informed of Jerry's passing, and it was tragic news to our family. You will be missed Mr. Reiner, I forever thank you for your wisdom.

Another couple that played an invaluable role in my childhood and my life is the Boyds. Mr. Gary and Ms. Diana are as close to me as any aunt and uncle that I've ever known. I will never forget the amazing times I've had with them over the years; cookouts, pool parties, country club functions, recording studios, golf outings, mining adventures and Ajo Al's until we've popped. I appreciate you both for all you've done, and I hope you know how truly special you are to me.

My sister and I were blessed with an "adopted grandpa" named Dave Davis. Since both of my Grandfathers had passed, he stepped in and spoiled us like we were his own. New bikes, NASCAR races, homemade Swedish pancakes and camping trips are only a few of my fond memories of Grandpa Dave. We are lucky to all be back in Arizona now so that we can see him and his wife Joyce on a regular basis. Thank you for all the help you've given me, and all the fun you've shared.

I have also been blessed with a fantastic extended family, and unfortunately, I don't get to see them as much as I would like to. Most memorably, my Aunt Charla needs to be recognized because everyday she explodes with energy, creativity, and an overwhelming, infectious appetite for laughter. In my 31 years of life, Aunt Charla, no matter where she's lived, has never missed a holiday. We always get a nicely wrapped box with gifts inside, and we always know from whom it came, because her handwriting is known throughout the world from the correspondence that she maintains. Without fail, she tracks us down with gifts each year, always knowing the proper sizes and wish lists, etc. This is an amazing feat when you consider that we move all the time, and hardly ever see her. She has a wonderful smile, a loving heart and a brilliant mind. Aunt Charla, I appreciate the interest you've always shown in my life, I love you.

If I made a list of all the people that were important to me, and all of the people that have inspired me along the way, we'd need 200 more pages. Thank you all.

LOVE

This poem's a token
Of love that I send

This poem's a gift
To my dearest of friends

To the neighbors that watched
As I grew day by day

That now see me work
But remember my play

To my family so scattered
All over this land

That I don't see much
Yet they still understand

My wants and desires
My hopes and my dreams

They know what I'm thinking
At least, so it seems

From my earthly connections
To all things above

This poem's for you
And I send it with love.

LOST

Alone in the world like when somebody leaves you
With nothing to say because no one believes you

You try to look forward but keep looking back
Where the sins of your past have diverged your life's track

You know where you're going, and where you have gone
You keep looking back like you'll never go on

It's time to let go, of the past that is burning
And look to the future, your scarred heart is yearning

But why did this happen? How'd you get this way?
Did you think it couldn't get better someday?

Did no one tell you of the place you can't hide?
Where you're always at home and you're welcome inside

This place is your soul; it's a place you possess
Your pain can be healed by its gentle caress

So never refrain now from looking within
This power of love might just save you again

And in the direction that's right, you will turn
And pages of bad times gone by, you will burn.

AS I REMEMBER GRANDMA

As memories swell inside my heart, with paper and my pen
I'll try to put my feelings down as I remember when
As I remember Grandma's rag, she'd bathe me in her tub
No water from a shower-head would come from up above

And also I remember, every birthday from my past
When Grandma'd make a perfect cake, so good, it wouldn't last
And in this world, you haven't lived, until you've had the chance
To eat biscuits and gravy, 'til you broke out of your pants

I feel so very lucky that my Grandma's been a part
Of travels that will always keep a smile within my heart.
As I remember Grandma in so many different places
I see her in my mind's eye, with my family's smiling faces

She added so much fun, to all our trips around the world
Our favorite traveling partner, she'd be ready in a whirl
Hawaii's beaches tamed her, but she didn't brave the tide
She isn't yet a swimmer, so from water she would hide

Until we took a long sea cruise, and she was quite the sport
She rode atop the waves as we saw gorgeous island ports
Puerto Rico, then Jamaica, we shopped until we dropped
The Caymans, Costa Rica, cruise ships fed us 'til we popped

The Panama Canal, a giant feat of man's creation
Was even that much better, watching Grandma's adulation
I can't put into words, how much my Grandma means to me
She's always there to talk to, and her heart is warm and sweet
So I wish you happy birthday, through my memories, smiles and tears
I pray you'll join our travels for another eighty years.

Happy 80th Birthday Grandma!

Thanks for being the greatest Grandmother
that anyone could ever hope to have.
You've made my life special, and I love you.

December 25, 2000

BLINDING

I know you don't feel loved right now
And though this is untrue

I thought I'd tell the truth right now
And say that I love you

Inside my heart of many loves
By giving life to rhyme

Your being dominates my soul
With you I am sublime

I need to know you love me
And I need to know you care

I need for you to understand
That I am always there

I hope you know the past does not
Give rise to all that be

For we have given up old fights
To deal with you and me

Because we have just one short life
To get this all done right

So I profess my love for you
So bright, it blinds my sight.

BUILT TO LAST?

His mind released distraction
But his heart still feels the pain

He lies awake in agony
His heart still feels the same

Once atop the mountain
Where he used to rule the land

Girls and money courted him
In castles made of sand

But now his world has crumbled
And his kingdom's lost control

The water takes his footprints
As the tide surrounds his soul

The joy he's had has ended
And the lives he's led have passed

The sorrow from the lies he's told
Have built a pain to last.

WALK THE LINE

We're here to watch you cross that stage
Your campus time is through

Four years I've watched you study
Now you're on to something new

Today I join with family
And with all your friends from class

To wish you well in all you do
You've grabbed that ring of brass

And as you go into this world
A blessing you'll become

For, as a student you've prepared
For all that's soon to come

Curriculum in excess,
More exams than I would want

Have made you one fine student
As you make this little jaunt

No matter where you study
You'll shine bright like glowing sun

So study hard, but don't forget
You still deserve your fun

My friend, you now must say goodbye
To college and the times

God bless the newest members
Of this class that walks the line.

DISCOVER CHIROPRACTIC

Before man walked the landscapes
And before life found dis-ease

Innate brought forth perfection
In the oceans, lakes and trees

The skies of blue and fields of green
The creatures great and small

This world of planned intelligence
Has given life to all

As rivers made of nerves still flow
Through all the things that be

We strive to keep these streams alive
One art has found the key

The art to help your body heal
This science that we learn

Philosophy we understand
For wellness, all shall yearn

So take the key, unlock the door
Remove unhealthy strife

Discover Chiropractic-
For a happy, healthy life.

EXTINCTION

Across the darkest continent
These victims roam the land

White ones die, and blacks do too
No, I speak not of man

A horn God made to add protection
Mothers aide their young

The armor life provided
Cannot stop the poacher's gun

An all out war is underway
One army fights, not two

For harmless, loving Rhinos
Seek no vengeance on this coup

I share this tale of those in-danger
Nearing their demise

Beware of those that we endanger
Extinction tears their eyes.

FANTASTIC AT FIFTY

Nearly half a century, has come my father's way
It's fifty years of greatness that we celebrate today

He started out in '49, a brother and a son
He then became a husband, and a father full of fun

But in between, his roles were many, teacher, coach and guide
Pizza owner, vacation roamer, thirst for life inside

Cave wiring, scuba diving, a million tees to green
He also makes the finest clubs, a golfer's ever seen

Many have been fortunate, to know him all his life
But three I know are luckiest, his boy, his girl, his wife

We get him more than anyone, the weekends, trips, and home
He's always there for family time, in person, heart, or phone

He's never met a stranger, a hardy handshake and a smile
His personality so rare, his stories heard for miles

The greatest man I've ever known, he's meant the world to me
So, happy birthday daddy, I pray 50 more you'll see!

April 28, 1999

FLAT TIRE

I'm sorry that I said such things
My tongue that stung like bees

I'm sorry for your treatment
So I'm down upon my knees

To ask for your forgiveness
And to vow my love to you

Forever I will try to be
The man you want me to

So love me like you used to now
And hold me in your heart

As one you want to live with
So we'll never be apart

And pray we make this journey
With no wreck, or stupid spat

I will not drive through life like this
On tires, worn and flat.

THE TIMES

Feeling for the sufferers
My work continues on

My faith in my accomplishments
Prevents my passing on

Of all the help that's needed
In a world that falls so fast

I strive to keep in stride
With all the lives within my past

I patch my path to glory
Binding present goals with suture

That lead to steady fusion
In the time's unsteady future

And so my job is growing
And my time is drawing near

Where time is of the essence
And the world is full of fear

Fear of all the mystery
That causes pain through stigma

A world where straightest answers
Often drown within enigma

Though straining for exception
Still I pray that times will pass

But forced to face reality
I pray my nerves can last.

I have always loved politics, and when I moved to Atlanta for Chiropractic school, I knew that I wanted to make our university the best place on earth to get an education, so I immediately got involved with student government.

I was lucky enough to be the President of my class, for the entire four years that we were there. My officers and I were once invited to the home of Dr. Sid Williams, Founder and President of Life University. A true legend, and a visionary in Chiropractic, it was an honor to share conversation with him and his wife Dr. Nell in their warm surroundings.

That day I realized, that humans, as small and fragile as they may seem on this big green ball, can touch countless lives with their dreams, and their vision. If you have something to share with the world, share it, the next person may not have the courage to step up and make a difference.

FIREPLACE PHILOSOPHY

A perfect, rare occasion
Took place just the other day

An invite to the Williams' home
Was passed along our way

With hope and admiration
For this family and their goals

We felt so warm and welcomed
By their hearts, their minds and souls

A living legend spoke to us
His home, his dreams, his wife

A husband and his partner
Shared a speech of love for Life

Their trophies line the walls in home
Their minds fulfilled with story

Their hearts are filled with triumph
For their past has held such glory

Their love for all humanity
A bold undying vision

Have carved the way for us to learn
This path, now our decision

We thank you for your warmth and time
We thank you for your sharing

We pray that you may understand
You've blessed us with your caring.

UNDYING PASSION

Alive again with passion
Piece by piece fell into place

Ablaze was my desire
Every time I saw her face

The past had ceased to matter
And the future held no harm

The present was my one concern
As she lay in my arms

Memories of a long lost love
Now flowed into my mind

I hadn't felt this type of warmth
In quite the longest time

A feeling that should never end
Was back with me to stay

This feeling in the first place
Should have never gone away

Simply too good to be true
Is how this evening seems

I close my eyes and cherish
As this passion fills my dreams.

LAST TRIAL

Threads of your misfortune
Form a bond, like mesh, they braid
Life unfolds as life began
Our edges worn and frayed

Torn and tattered bodies
Take their stand to coming fate
Hopeless as they shake the hand
Of death, for he won't wait

And years of past flash-forward
In a whirlwind blur of light
A blitzkrieg of your life's events
Have you done wrong or right?

Your judgment is upon you
And at best, you fear the worst
You strive to recall anything
To quench your jury's thirst

The time you helped that sweet old man
Put groceries in his car
Or changed that tire in traffic
So that lady could go far

You pray that as you're audited
They see the good you've done
Your work in life's accomplishments
Mistakes, heartbreaks, and fun

For life's comprised of options
Chances to succeed are great
So if you feel you'll come up short
Start now, don't hesitate

Make positive that when time comes
And fate reviews your file
You've done something you're proud of
Live your life for that last trial.

MY SISTER'S GLOW

Let me introduce her now
For those who may not know

Her given name is Keri Tish
But you can call her "glow"

She glows with warmth and passion
In most everything she'll do

She strives to care for others
For her heart is full of truth

She shows her loving nature
In the only smile she knows

A smile that she shares freely
For her life explains her glow

Two parents that support her
And her brother loves her so

A dog that needs her touch
And all the kids that she'll watch grow

She's special in her special way
Her unique soul's a blessing

You'll see this in her own beliefs
Her style and in her dressing

A girl who works to help and love
Who gives, and won't say no

This Keri is a special friend
Her love, her warmth, her glow.

KToslin, I've loved you since the day you were born.

THANKS FOR THE MEMORIES

I've had some time to stop a while
Reflecting on this place

And how my caring parents
Helped create my perfect space

On every wall I see some-thing
My mother helped me hang

And still I hear my father's drill
And hear the hammer's bang

My mom and I made countless trips
The stores, the shops, the malls

And dad and I had too much fun
With Frisbees, darts and balls

Extra paint, new couch pillows
Tables, chairs and more

They even put a small white shelf
Behind the pantry door

I'm so glad, when I look around
It's not too hard to see

I'm thankful for my parents
For, they're just too good to me.

In my 31 years on this planet, I have witnessed some wonderful things and like many, have also been witness to tragedy.

On September 11, 2001, I think we all witnessed the worst tragedy that many of us had ever been exposed to. I wasn't alive during World War I or II, and I wasn't around when JFK was assassinated, and until this point, I think the most horrible thing I remember was the Space Shuttle Challenger explosion.

Everybody has a, *you'll always remember where you were when*, moment, well, this is mine, and it stung for a long time.

That September, when a cowardly terrorist took the lives of 3000 innocent people, my outlook on this world of ours changed dramatically.

No longer was the world filled with warm fuzzies, the world was now a playground for violent idealists that had a vicious point to prove. Sure they've always been out there, but now with modern technology, it was easier for them to harm the unsuspecting, and the undeserving. We have to learn that opposition to our way of life has always been there, and it always will be. We can't divert our path, because someone else wants us to, only when WE want to, is that acceptable.

This poem is a tribute to the heroes and victims that risked, sacrificed or lost their lives on that horrible day. My blessings and prayers go out to all of their families.

The bottom line is this; we cannot live in fear of what we can't see. We need to make this life the best life we can for ourselves, and for those around us. The power lies within us all to start each new day and live it to the fullest, to live it like it's our last.

Live because you can, and fight for your beliefs because you live.

No regrets.

HERE COMES THE EAGLE

A planet goes around and round, ideals change with the times
A plane has crashed without a sound, below we stare like mimes
In awe, we look to heaven, as the fire still burns within
Its awkward how it seems so real, I'd swear I'm sleeping in

A nightmare is unfolding, right before my crying eyes
Like lightening now, as three more planes have fallen from our skies
Rescue crews, with fearless souls, march straight into harms way
Though thousands scream in terror, they've got just one thing to say

'Are you alright, how can I help?' Entombed in doomed Twin Towers
And without warning, both crash down, foundations lose their power
Now lost among the ruins, women, children, men and more
Police and Fire *hero* crews, lay trapped, but why? What for?

A man who wore a suit to work, a lady in a dress
Did they unleash this hatred? Was it us who caused this mess?
No, these were just the victims, thousands gone with no remorse
So now we form a system, millions stand a steadfast course

Resolve to end this tragedy, restore our solemn creed
Dissolve this evil clan, we must, our world will share this deed
An enemy without a face, lay hiding in their caves
For as they tried to take ours, it's *their* freedom we'll enslave

But from these acts of violence, an *eagle* flew unscathed
A statue still stands proudly, she defends us still today
And in our darkest hour, from the concrete, smoke and steel
Our nation lends a helping hand, a warmth the whole world feels

It makes us even prouder, as we fly old glory high
To know what each thread represents, to know the reasons why
America so strong and proud, will rise from New York's dust
Then faith will be restored along with virtue, hope and trust.

God Bless those who lost their lives, and their loved ones
on that fateful September day.

ASTRONOMICAL EFFORTS

Blasting through the atmosphere
Their goal is outer space

It's one small step for someone
Leaps and bounds for human race

Booster rockets, asteroids
Planets stars and moons

A voyage that began just now
Will have them home so soon

Mankind stops for no one
Our technology is strong

A space program of monster feats
Has formed a record long

For those in zero-gravity
Enjoy your time from home

Remember us on planet earth
You're far, but not alone.

YES I & I

The truest, true SOUL REBEL
As he sways his NATTY DREAD
While the sweetest SONGS OF FREEDOM
Keep an irie vibe ahead

A RASTAMAN VIBRATION
There's a SOUL SHAKEDOWN in store
The fighting led to EXODUS
The hatred led to WAR

JAH LIVES inside his glowing heart
Sellassie in his soul
To LIVELY UP YOURSELF
Make faith in Jah your only goal

Jah children, GET UP–STAND UP
Heed the vital words he wrote
Make your message clear, oh system please
DON'T ROCK MY BOAT

Just STIR IT UP, make TRENCHTOWN ROCK
CRAZY BALDHEADS feel your pain
Unless you speak your heart and mind
We're all WAITING IN VAIN

WHO THE CAP FIT, they asked us
Like a well worn leather glove
NO WOMAN, NO CRY, this he sang
For he had just ONE LOVE

THREE LITTLE BIRDS pitched by his step
Like him, they sang REDEMPTION SONG
This prophet spoke in poetry
Still heard inside TUFF GONG.

MOTHER CHRISTMAS

A mother kind and caring
A dear, most perfect wife
A soul that gave her love to me
And also gave me life

From little league, piano woes
Karate and guitar
To skateboards and my ten-speed bike
The Bronco, my first car

My mother stood close by my side
Support was all she gave
She backed me at the TPC
And helped at Mammoth Cave

She stood by me in times of trouble
Times I needed love
She guided me in worship
Of the glory held above.

Weekends, summers, holidays
The breaks, and graduations
My fondest memories with my mom
Have come while on vacations

I can't explain this gratitude
To re-pay, I could never
I share a Merry Christmas
And a love I'll have forever.

POWDER KING

The snow like powdered sugar
Crunched beneath my sharpened skis

Bundled in my gear, so warm
With nylon, wool and fleece

Along the sheer white hillside
Ant-like skiers peppered snow

The ski lift offered transport
To the summit of our goal

Atop the mystic mountain
Certain majesty ran wild

I lost my fear and listened
To my wandering inner child

I raced the edge of madness
Down the slopes of endless fun

The last man on the mountain
I was king of that last run.

THE GREAT FLOOD

The world is ever changing,
But the flowers cease to grow
Since Mother Nature's children
Cause more damage than they know

Society is falling
And our wildlife slowly drops
Politicians stalling
As the farmers lose their crops

Government officials
Just stand by to watch the pain
While God does all that he can do
To send the farmers rain

The poachers of this world-
Erase a future proud and strong
Those certain helpless species
Live a life that won't last long

And criminals escaping
Due to faulty locks on doors
But why escape with three square meals
Plush carpet on the floors

The evil of this world
Still get the praise the good deserve
And nothing for our proud police
They help, protect and serve

Our planet's size is growing
As our ignorance explodes
A journey to seek righteousness
Should flood our nation's roads.

PERFECT LIFE
For Tony and Mary Beth

As sunsets fall, and moonbeams rise
Perfection's found its place

A smile of truest happiness
Spread 'cross this couple's face

A girl with golden hair
With eyes to light a darkened room

A man whose heart is made of gold
A loving, caring groom

A love has found a home in them
A life has just set sail

An ocean of eternity
Holds all that dreams entail

May God look down upon these two
And bless this perfect life

For, here's the perfect man
To match this shining, perfect wife.

My great aunt is one of the main reasons I became a Chiropractor. She nearly died with kidney failure in her youth, when Dr. Hill, a young Chiropractor in Kentucky, worked with her through the night, saving her life.

As you can tell by this poem, she lived well into her years, passing gracefully, just a few months shy of 100!

LILIAN

Happy Birthday Lilian,
Your ninety-five today

And we are filled with joy,
That we could celebrate this way

So nice to have you here today,
So nice to be with you

We wish you all the best
Our love and wishes strong and true

So as you blow the candles out,
Thank God for what's in store

Because we'll all be praying,
That you have a hundred more!

WHO'S THIS GIRL?

I never thought this day would come
But now we must begin
You've left me no choice gorgeous
For, the poems are back again

I walked back in my room today
And someone made my bed
Then through my foggy tired mind
These thoughts ran through my head

Who's this girl I'm craving here?
Who's this girl I love?
Who's this girl that fills my soul
Like sunshine from above?

She's not right then, she's not right now
She's right in every way
She always knows what things to do
And just what words to say

Two Cardinal's fans, two tickets and-
Her wardrobe's now been planned
They'll hear us shout together
As we're screaming from the stands

It warms my heart to know in time
She'll make me smile in life
It makes me proud to picture this
My perfect, fun-filled wife

So who's this girl I'm raving for?
And who's this poem to?
That girl that rules my every thought?
She's heaven sent, she's you!

BEEZIE

A life so full of happiness, a laugh that wouldn't rest
A heart of love to share with you, our Beezie was the best

When sitting with the TV on, may no one touch that dial
Still nothing but her Channel Five could bring forth such a smile

With high heel shoes on both her feet, a Coke can in her hand
She'd board that big blue Chevrolet, and drive across the land

To only add a couple miles, that Chevy had so few
She'd be the first, so proud of course, to share that fact with you

A happy, cheerful person, oh how Ken and Jane took care
With pictures of her loved ones, our Aunt Beezie often shared

Katie, Tyler, Chris and Keri, Kevin and Mike in frame
Her neighbors watched us grow through film; our lives won't be the same

But sadness has escaped me, now she's in a better place
I won't forget her funny pranks, or smiles upon her face

So many lives she touched on earth, with passion deep and true
We'll miss you dearest Beezie, rest in peace, for we love you.

My Aunt Beezie was a truly unique individual with an amazing zest for life!

MATH 113

This math class is the lowest
Like the lint beneath our feet

Consumed and dazed in total loss
When I sit in this seat

I might as well just give up now
There simply is no use

It's wasting parent's money
As I take this cold abuse

I'm gonna fail the next three tests
And all his quizzes too

But I can't say it's some surprise
Fail math is what I do.

SILVER ANNIVERSARY

A Silver Anniversary
A precious time for love

A day to give your thanks to Him
For blessings from above

For, since June 1970
So many things you've done

Many goals you've conquered
With your many battles won

An obvious compassion
And a true undying heart

Has formed a love inside you both
So you will never part

I'm proud of your accomplishments
Since you've been groom and wife

But from the bottom of my heart
I thank you for my life.

Happy 25th mom and dad!

June 7, 1995

South-Central Kentucky is cave country. The area is loaded with caves because of what geologists call a *karst topography*. (I just put that in there for my caving buddies, I'd say only a very small percentage of people actually know, or even care what that term means).

My family was always around the caves, in fact, my parents once owned and operated a private show cave called Diamond Caverns, a few miles from Mammoth Cave National Park. DiamondCaverns.com will show you beautiful pictures, and tell the history of this magnificent, and beautiful cave that was such an important part of my childhood.

Mammoth Cave is the longest cave in the world at 346 miles. Just imagine something longer than the Grand Canyon with layers of honeycombed tunnels, and a lid on it, it's simply amazing. Spelunkers have currently mapped almost 350 miles of existing cave passageway, and more is yet to come. Think about that for a second, 350 miles of explored cave! If you have never been to Mammoth Cave, I highly recommend it.

If you fancy a journey, set your sights for Park City, Kentucky, gateway to Mammoth Cave National Park, hence the name PARK City. Believe it or not, my great-grandfather Dr. Elwood Rowsey actually coined the name "Park City." Once called Glasgow Junction, when the Mammoth Cave area became a recognized park, so changed the name. Tours began in 1816, and Congress voted to make the area surrounding the cave a National Park in 1926. The only park that is any older is Niagara Falls, but as you can guess, it may have been a little easier to find. Visit NPS.gov to learn more, or simply show up at the park and ask for Foxy Joe, he's always happy to lend a helping hand.

A record holding, fifth-generation interpreter at the Park, I worked at Mammoth Cave in the summer of 1993, as a seasonal guide while attending the University of Kentucky. Members of the McDaniel family, most recently myself, have taken visitors through Mammoth Cave since 1857. My father Vernon, grandfather Martie, great-grandfather Joe, and great-great grandfather Dabney, took thousands of tourists through Mammoth Cave, many before the Cave itself was even recognized as a part of the National Park system in 1941. Mammoth Cave, Kentucky is a beautiful area with tons of amazing history, and I hope that you will visit there when you can.

I am sad to say that I never knew my namesake Martie McDaniel, but through my dad, my loving grandfather still guides me.

THIS WORLD BELOW

Another world exists today
Not one most people know
A privilege held by very few
To learn of what's below

Cease to see the life up top
And follow in the dark
A journey to the underworld
Is ready to embark

We delve into the cave's unknown
Rooms *mammoth* in their size
The walls are telling stories
Some tell truth and some tell lies

Events remain mysterious
You simply must believe
The past, and all that *rambles* here
Are hard to still conceive

A million years of passage
Fossils, torches, bones, and more
Have made this world a priceless one
As treasures line the floor

Mountains, canyons, rivers, streams
My new world has it all
And through the massive darkness
In this world, I'm less than small

Species of some animals
Not seen atop the earth
Have lived inside these caverns
Since the river's mighty birth

No man could ever learn the lot
Of all there is to know
So in our dying ignorance
Protect this world below.

SEEDS TO GROW

As mother sews my worn-out clothes
My father sews the land

Spreading for a harvest
From the grain that leaves his hand

Growth from faith and knowledge
From our souls, like from the ground

The silence of the sewing seed
Is quite the deafening sound

As we approach this harvest
With the spreading of the word

We must ensure our farmers dear
That we'll protect the dirt

Allowing peaceful growing
Without falter, without end

The body spreads the seeds
So that the spirit may ascend.

ABSENCE

Absence makes the heart grow fonder
So that's what they say

But did the man who coined it
Ever need to go away

And leave a precious soul behind
So perfect and so dear

Who said that distance from your love
Would bring your lover near?

I don't believe I understand
And still I won't agree

This phrase explaining loneliness
As what a man should be

Of course an absence does have end
Some near and sometimes never

But when and where that next one comes
I hope it takes forever.

Since I could remember, I wanted to be a Kentucky Wildcat. When I finally graduated high school in Arizona, I made the trek back to Lexington to embark on an amazing journey, filled with countless memories, and dozens of life long friendships.

I was a student at UK at such a wonderful time. I took the pre-med coursework, and also majored in Psychology. To avoid working too hard, I gladly went on the five-year plan. A campus loaded with tradition and beauty, I couldn't have chosen a better place to attend college. We were recently graced with the recognition of having "The Basketball Team of the Century". Seven National Championships and thousands of tournament wins, we are unmatched in the NCAA, and have the highest winning percentage of any program in college sports.

My senior year, 1996, our basketball team won the National Championship. Think about that, of all the kids, in all the schools, only a handful were able to say that their school won it all during their senior year. Luckily for me and my five-year plan, we went back to the Final Four in '97 and I was fortunate enough to go to the game in Indianapolis. So, I was able to be on campus during the excitement of winning it all in '96, and then actually attended a National Championship game the next year.

As you may know, Kentucky is not a football powerhouse, but our quarterback during my time there, Tim Couch, was chosen as the number one pick in the NFL draft right after I left.

I never missed a home game in football or basketball, and a group called the B-2 Bombers even attended some away games with me; Indiana, Tennessee, Louisville, etc. The occasional road trip was a welcome addition to our studies. If it's good enough for Ashley Judd, then being life-long, blue-blooded fans was good enough for us, and still is today.

I loved my time in the Bluegrass so much, that when I moved back to Scottsdale, I founded the UK Alumni Club of Arizona, which is linked to the National alumni association. I am still the President of the organization here, representing over 1200 Kentucky graduates living in the Valley of the Sun.

Go Cats!

GO BIG BLUE

Kentucky Wildcats Basketball
The games, the fans, the past
Tradition of a well-loved team
Has built a pride to last

From Robey, Givens, Issel, Farmer
Chapman, Dampier, Casey
To Mashburn, Dent, today's cats too
With broadcast by Kyle Macy

The three-point bombs, and monster dunks
Get cat fans wild in Rupp
With Coach Pitino's sideline dance
We just can't get enough

So all the home games get my view
I'll never miss a one
Away games pose no threat to us
We'll get our best job done

You can't explain the common bond
Of those in blue and white
They cheer at Rupp, they cheer at home
Support with all their might

Commending cat fans everywhere
I'm glad our spirit reigns
This poem is for the wildcat fans
With blue blood in their veins

Our fight song carries loudly
From the Bluegrass to the shore
I'll see you at the season's end
At this year's Final Four

So from my Old Kentucky Home
With colors, proud and true
I lend my voice when cheering here
Forever GO BIG BLUE!

FOREVER AND ALWAYS

I once was alone, 'til I wished on that star
I knew you were out there but now here you are

I've searched a whole lifetime, and no one I've found
Could equal your feelings, your touch and your sound

The words that you use, and the things that you say
You make me thank God that I've got you each day

We can only blame fate on the fact we're in love
But still I am grateful, to all that's above

I was given a treasure to have and to hold
When it's in my arms, I can feel nothing cold

My girl is the warmth that I've needed to feel
With the love and compassion I need to be real

So now with a love that is perfect and true
I want you to know that my treasure is you

As much as I love you, and in all that I say
I still must remind you, each night and each day

This poem is yours to help you understand
Forever and always, that I'll be your man.

SURVIVAL

People are people, all over this world
No matter what they say

We all still share a common dream
We each live day to day

From those who walk the streets at night
To those in fancy cars

From those who make the laws that guide
To those behind the bars

And don't forget the crying babies
Lonely through the night

And all the trying mothers there
Who set their dreams in flight

From homeless children everywhere
A life no one deserves

To those who throw their scraps away
And those who show the nerve

From those without compassion
Who won't help us to survive

A dying population lives
So we might start to thrive.

Luckily, I had some connections in the registrar's office that helped me achieve this little task. At our graduation ceremony, this poem was rolled into the makeshift scroll that each graduate received as they shook Dr. Sid's hand, while walking across the stage. What a great way for me to actually "touch" the other fledgling Chiropractors on a day that we had worked so hard to achieve.

I wish my classmates the best, and hope that they are all doing well, and helping people every day.

TODAY, I AM A CHIROPRACTOR

I woke up in a dream today
And God looked down on me

His voice was loud like thunder
His message clear as clear could be

He told me that each man on earth
Is given just one chance

To use their skills for goodness
Not the thrills of happenstance

He mentioned all the scientists
Their inventing, and their theories

He talked about the Audubon
Sears Tower, and World Series

He gave us mighty oceans
Therefore, fishermen we need

And land that still provides for us
As farmers work their seed

The final words he spoke then
Filled my heart with warmth and pride

He told me he was thankful
Of these gifts we have inside

He said that we could help mankind
In different loving ways-

Then said, "Son you're a Chiropractor
That's how you'll help today."

June 17, 2001

CAVE CITY FIVE-O

We gather here this evening
At the Diamond Cavern's lot
The perfect celebration
Of a day that's not forgot

A day that blessed his mom and dad
And later, child and wife
A date back 50 years ago
The day he started life

JBM, as you may know
If known at all, is Jimmy
A friend to all he meets
And those he helps are numbered plenty

Glenda makes his perfect home
As they've watched Sarah grow
His hobbies wide and varied
Maybe some you didn't know

He rides like ole Roy Rogers
And he's raised a million cows
Learned to fly an airplane
Placed employees through the town

He dabbles in artesian wells
With Calvert Spring in tow
The man's dove more Deep Ocean
Than the late, great Jacques Cousteau

Atop it all, his greatest skill
How he treats fellow man
Sincere, and full of kindness
Always there to lend a hand

So to the greatest family friend
To ever come our way
We wish you all the best
Here at your 50th Birthday.

KEY TO HAPPINESS

Within the realm of happiness
Exists a single thought

To do the things you like to do
Acceptable or not

Accomplishing the goals you've made
And reaching all your dreams

To bring success still closer
Ever distant may it seem

Clouds of dismal offering
Lay low around your head

Your mind reminds you daily
Of the things your heart has said

Pushing you to strive your hardest
Failure falls behind

To be the best at what you do
In all of humankind

Hence, the key to happiness
Those things your dreams entail

So if your dreams are fleeting fast
Success shall hold your stare.

NOT THE ONE

Not quite understanding
Why you try to build my pain
Breaking down this wall I've built
Please stop my eyes that rain

My soul cannot convince my mind
To go without you now
I thought that something special
Could be here, somewhere, somehow

But then you throw my world away
Add hurting to my life
The loneliness of sad despair
Has now become my strife

A memory of the times gone by
Still rise like morning sun
I must explain to heart within
You must not be the one

Not the one to hold me
When embrace is what I need
And not the one to guide me
For your words, I used to heed

Its better to have lost a love
Than not to love at all
With bricks of trust and time's cement
I must rebuild this wall.

A BATTLE LOST

Waking from a revelation
Clouds now fill my mind

Reaching final expectation
Lost by humankind

No one really understanding
Battles still rage on

Constant useless reprimanding
No one here has won

A solemn lie, protecting lives
At any price or cost

For no one that this world deprives
Shall win this battle lost.

In 1995, my favorite band, Oingo Boingo, disbanded after almost twenty years together. I was fortunate enough to attend a pre-concert party with the band before the Las Vegas venue of their farewell tour. My friends and I were able to hand the following poem to the band before they hit the stage. In appreciation of the poem, they sent an autographed photo that still hangs on my wall today.

Since the break-up, the talented lead singer, and primary songwriter, Danny Elfman has gone on to compose some of the greatest scores in Hollywood. Boingo fans of the world know that through a dozen albums of material, his lyrics spoke to just as many people as his film-music does.

Danny once wrote a song called *Out of Control*, for a friend that had contemplated suicide. In that respect, I hope that my poetry speaks to people that need it, just as his songs did.

The stories in his music helped make me the poet I am today.

MYSTIC KNIGHTS OF THE OINGO BOINGO

The Mystic knights have reigned supreme
For nearly twenty years
The Oingo Boingo's aura
Will not fall with all our tears

For in a vision far away
Where sunlight seldom shines
The distance of the traveled space
Was lost within the times

A lonesome band of scattered souls
Create their own true breed
Where inner thoughts and feelings
Form a strong and sacred creed

A creed that we have lived by
And a creed that we will teach
To those in our *Society*
Our voices in their reach

The lyrics tell the story
Of the lives an Elfman led
Now Boingo must retreat
And we must put the ghost to bed

Their darkness will encompass us
Their songs will take us over
The flip-side of reality
Will rest upon our shoulders

Thank you for the Dead Man's Parties
Thank you for your souls
Thank you for your music
And the magic that it holds

Since, *No One Lives Forever*
Loyal fans, no need to cry
As Boingo's call is blessing us
For now, *Goodbye-Goodbye.*

ABOVE

Ablaze amidst the moonlit sky
My love inside's like fire

The strength from which my heart endows
Allows me not to tire

Expressing simple movements
And explaining certain thoughts

Capturing the special ones
That most times can't be caught

By sharing both the memories
Of past and present too

And loving all the happenstance
That's made me fall for you

My love for you shines brightly
Like the stars that glow above

My faith in your perfection
Is now equaled by my love.

ONE ENCHANTED EVENING

A warm stare from across the room
Has landed in my sights

A glance to show some interest
And an offer to entice

As mystery engulfs the air
I wonder what she's thinking

I want to taste the food she eats
And smell the mix she's drinking

As suddenly my dream approaches
Here, where I now stand

I greet her and she smiles at me
I then extend my hand

The stranger from my age-old dream
Has placed her hand in mine

I've longed to look into those eyes
Caress that hair so fine

For on this blessed evening
I have seen my dreams come true

A love tonight has blossomed
In a world that spares so few.

My family and I have been lucky in life, and blessed to know some amazing people, and do some amazing things. We have been to all fifty states, as a family. We have traveled to nearly a hundred countries, as a family. Trains, planes, automobiles, helicopters, and ships are only a few of our favorite modes of travel, not to mention, parachutes, scuba gear, kayaks, white water rafts, and more. We have met hundreds of celebrities, and have seen some of the most unforgettable sights on God's green earth.

I would venture to say, and I speak for the whole family here, that nothing beats coming home, and no celebrity is more interesting than a regular, small town family friend.

I have learned that life is a funny ride, with a different meaning for everyone. Your greatest journey may be to your favorite restaurant with your family. Your favorite vacation may be a trip to the zoo with your kids. The biggest stars in your life may be the people that live right down your street, and not the people in the tabloid magazines.

We are immensely blessed because we have been able to share our lives with memorable people that you will never see on the silver screen, and visit them in places that most people can't even find on a map.

One of those great families for us is the Robbins clan of Auburn, KY. They are a wonderfully fabulous couple that has been close to us as long as I've been alive. She's a classic beauty, and he's a true southern gentleman. They've been together over fifty years, and he still opens every door for her, and she gets dressed to the nines just to have a cup of coffee.

This poem was a gift for them at their fiftieth wedding anniversary. May you all be blessed with the likes of such wonderful friends.

A DECEMBER TO REMEMBER

Oh how I wish that I could be
Among you all tonight

To share congratulations
With the two who've done it right

Our loyal friends and family know
That all across this land

There still exists no couple
With the warmth they have at hand

Ken and Mary Jane, you see
Were wed in fair December

A flash just fifty years ago
But, oh how they remember

The fun, the sun, the tears and cheers
In Auburn, their new home

With outstretched hands they settled there
And never were alone

Perfect parents raised their boys
As Mike and Kevin grew

Their grandchildren now bless this clan
And they keep growing too

So with these words I want to share
My love and admiration

Fifty years of love and luck
Sincere congratulations.

December 21, 2002

ENDANGERED

With hair of sun drenched yellow
And the sea within her eyes

Eternal love from this sweet girl
Will come as no surprise

I cannot live without her
And I hope our time will last

Her warmth within my arm's embrace
Has buried all the past

I can't remember anything
Before I met my love

Reminded of her peacefulness
As eagles soar above

They're watching over everything
She watches over me

Determination's filling
As she sets her loving free

Like animals endangered
I will love her with my care

And like those sacred species
I would die if she weren't there.

A LESSON TO LEARN

It was special to me, simply one of a kind
When the loving was over, it dwelled on my mind

'Cause I lost the battle, in love's ugly war
But I just kept on fighting and don't know what for

A life-changing shame, how the love, it went bad
If you ponder like I did, its really quite sad

But what can you do when the love goes away
You now must accept it, love's game's hard to play

To me she's like someone forever I'd known
With countless close friends, without her, I'm alone

She's moved on without me, and left from my world
That's not what I wanted from that little girl

You never can tell what will happen to you
So give love you best, for it's all you can do

Just ante up once and you're never the same
Since no one made rules for your heart's deadly game

To her I'm an image, a memory to burn
Love's without fail, the worst lesson to learn.

OUR WORLD

Our world is such magic, a beautiful thing
From the bright colored birds to the songs that they sing

From high shining stars that glow in the night
To the soft-spoken words than can make it alright

From tall growing tree branches towered above
To kind, restless hearts that can power your love

From clear, untouched skies, ever cloudless throughout
To a soul that can show you what life's all about

From your mind that will guide you through good times and bad
To your tears that relieve you in times when you're sad

From nightmares at bedtime that often bring screams
To a world of amazement you'll find in your dreams

From the songs that can lift you, and keep you all day
To the words in those songs, that forever you'll say

From beautiful tunes that can make time go by
To the sadness in some that can make grown men cry

From the positive thoughts that can make you go on
When you know in your heart that someday we'll be one

To the truth in those thoughts, you see, life is a prize
May you never turn back, when the doubt fills your eyes.

LIFE'S BLOOD

A love as bright as firelight
Has poured itself on me

And through this drowning feeling
I can barely even see

The warmth flows over top of me
Like river's water warm

Unlike the things I've felt before
From evil's icy storm

So thank you all for showers
Of the love from which I breathe

And promise me forever
That my life's blood here won't leave.

While my parents both worked to provide for my sister and I, we received insurmountable help from the Tisdale and Duvall families of Park City, Kentucky.

Nannie May Tisdale helped my family on a daily basis, preparing meals and watching after us, while Joe and Louvenia Duvall also assisted us in every way you can imagine.

These two families truly helped raise us in those early years, and I feel our well-rounded youth and upbringing is directly related to the exposure we had to these varied, nurturing people. Thank you all for your influence in my life.

The following poem was written for Ms. Tisdale's 90th birthday. Unfortunately she passed a few years later, and will be greatly missed by her huge extended family.

CAREGIVER

This special person cared for me
When I was just a boy

A caring person shared with me
And smiled to lend her joy

Meals a king would love to eat
Prepared by loving hands

She gladly taught me right from wrong
Until I'd understand

This special person changed my life
In countless, timely ways

This special person's celebrating
Ninety years today

Bless you dear Ms. Tisdale
How I hope you're doing fine

I wish that I could be with you
To share this birthday rhyme.

IT IS MINE

Physical affliction
Like a cage around my soul

Has changed my life forever
With a curse I can't control

Conditions that will hinder me
And never change through time

A winding road that I must face
For this life, it is mine

CLASSROOM SURRENDER

I sit here in a hopeless gaze
My teacher's mouth keeps moving

I hear no words, I feel no touch
Nor taste the gum I'm chewing

A friend of mine now waits for me
A meal awaits us both

But keeping me from pleasure
Here, I'm lost in boring notes

To only have a shortened class
And exit to the hall

I'd give my whole life savings
For, I hear my dinner call

Statistics is the topic
In a battle she can't lose

My teacher puts the problem up
As I go down to snooze

Its twice a week, I get my nap
While lecture class goes on

And when the bell rings loud and clear
From this classroom I'm gone!

WITHOUT

On days when clouds are many
And the sky might hint at rain
I've always got my special love
To make those puddles drain

Her love is strong like Hercules
She'll never lose her heart
And as for times we'll spend, well spent
I hope we'll never part

At any time, of any day
She shames the sun's great light
Her eyes, her smell, her smile, her hair
She keeps me safe from fright

There's only one of her around
I'm thankful that she's mine
There's no need to continue
For no better will I find

Her eyes are pools of clarity
Reflections of her soul
With purity within her mind
To love her is my goal

To do my best, to try too hard
Then maybe I'll succeed
To equal all she's done for us
And all she's given me

So thank you much my beauty
You're the reason I'm alive
Without your love, within my heart
My heart would not survive.

HOPELESS

Without a hope inside
There is no spirit in my head
It's like an empty body
When the rest has not been fed

I just don't understand this time
The sun refused to shine
I know I want my life back
With a future to call mine.

BETRAYED BY THE OTHER

I can't explain the problem here, emotions uncontrolled
Have now begun to hurt me as this pain engulfs my soul
The friendships that I've worked for and the love I strived to gain
Have now been all but tainted as the *other* gives me pain

It's not to say she's out of place, and not that I don't care
But taking time from my short life, for nothing, isn't fair
So as I stand in disbelief, betrayal at my glance
I'd like to think I'm just the butt, of some joke's circumstance

But as I look down at my wrist, the time still flies; she's quick
As tick then turns to tock, I'm then informed that it's no trick
So troubles fast and furious still lie within my mind
To think that I'll escape this is the joke of all mankind

This problem is the here and now, I cannot turn my back
I must confess, not second-guess, as I stay well on track
But never have I been a fan of starting confrontation
For always in my past I've always hated altercation

Between a rock and hard place, I can't seem to understand
The feelings and emotions that I now see here at hand
Jesus won't you please help me, as I pray to you above
I cannot find the hatred, for it's buried by my love

But fairness is the factor that I'd pay to see in time
And guilt beneath my weeping makes me feel that it's a crime
For, when we started out, it seemed that all involved were friends
Now logically we can't return, the future must begin

And I'm not one to now believe that it's not *what* you know
What gets you far is *who*, not what, as time will surely show
And if this *other* knew the deal, I think she'd drop the ball
But if I spoke to her again, I might just lose it all

My situation must improve, acceptance here is needed
And when I've found the love once felt, I'll know that I've succeeded
But finally I must find peace, for now my battle's done
The whole thing shall remain a draw, for no one here has won.

THE MOVING PICTURE SHOW

Sometimes I dodge reality
And plan a quick retreat

To places you can't visit
Watching faces you can't meet

Escaping to a far off land
Or going back in time

I live through those on silver screens
Whose stars will always shine

A pirate one day I shall be
A super-hero next

A mighty wizard I'll become
While in this seat, I'm hexed

Where outer space is in my reach
And too, the ocean's deep

In movies you can see your dreams
Without the need for sleep.

This poem was written for a fabulous Chiropractor and friend in Bowling Green, Kentucky. I always admired his beautiful practice, and his kind, efficient office staff. From him, I learned that a trip to the doctor could actually be fun. When this poem was written, I was only a patient, and not yet a colleague, but hopefully I have made good on the influence of Dr. John G. Erskine.

BOOMERANG

A field that I'm in love with
Has produced a man who cares

And patients that adore him
Are the first who want to share

They tell of their successes
Both in body and in mind

For Dr. Erskine's skill
Has lent a hand to all mankind

See, what you need to visit him
Is not too hard to find

His only choice requirement:
You first must have a spine

So, if you meet this guideline
And you'd like to learn much more

Good health and smiles await you
When you walk through his front door.

PARROTHEADS

Jimmy Buffett's fans are one eclectic group of souls
An ageless group of fruitcakes that could never miss his shows

One harbor in particular, still calls the band their own
Where coral reefers back the only lead they've ever known

With Mike and Mac, and Robert too, they've "played" their dues in time
Without the skills this band fulfills, the *Mailboat's* bells won't chime

With barefoot rage upon that stage, his blue guitar's in tow
The hula skirts start swaying when the margaritas flow

A concert here, a café there, an empire in the making
A telegraph of coconuts has kept the palm trees shaking

They'll dance across the hemisphere, through rain and sleet and snow
For Tuesdays, Thursdays, Saturdays will bring a sold out show

No matter where you're sitting, from reserved seats, to the lawn
This carnival won't stop 'til all the parrotheads have gone.

Fins Up!

THE LOCKER

Mercury sinks as raindrops fall
Cold to colder, waves too tall

This stormy night is here to stay
If Davy Jones can have his way

The swells can tell, control's been lost
It matters not the seas you've crossed

An icy wind engulfs the sails
And pirate lore still fuels our tales

An ocean full of life and death
May help you take your last long breath

So fear the depth that waits below
If you can't stop his undertow

And pray the hull is strong and tight
So you can stay afloat tonight

Embrace the storm, and drift to sleep
Avoid your fate, the locker deep.

GRATITUDE

Much too long I think it's been
Too awfully long this time

Since I sat down with my blue pen
To send my love a rhyme

My heart would never beat again
My lungs would never rise

If I did not have all your love
Your heart, your soul, your eyes

So thank you for your loving touch
You keep me going strong

I hope the time you spend with me
Will make our love go long

For years and years, and decades too
I want you in my life

And someday soon I'll take your hand
Then you'll become my wife.

GOODBYE

I think our visit's over now
I guess its time to go

I don't believe I want to leave
Again, I just don't know

I really love to be here, see
It fills my heart with joy

There's only so much special care
A girl can give one boy

But maybe I'll just hold on tight
You know we both can try

I never want a reason, love
To say goodbye-goodbye.

This poem wasn't originally written to be the last page in my first poetry book, it was written because, for most of my life, I have hated the end of anything. When I was little, I hated the thought that we would all die someday, and that our time on earth was fleeting. Mom had a big talk with me using a little butterfly book, explaining that we human caterpillars one day become glorious butterflies. Later, I found that I still hated the end of anything, a concert, a movie, a good meal, a vacation, a friendship, a fun class, or summer camp. One of my favorite lines in any movie is in *Cocktail*, when Brian Flannegan's girlfriend says "I don't want it to end like this," and he says, "Everything ends badly, otherwise it wouldn't end." I always thought that was so prophetic, and again, I always avoided the end, of everything.

As I have grown older, (older, not up) I have realized that when one door closes, a hallway of doors opens, and when one facet of life ends, a new, amazing journey can begin. Without change, we can't possibly fulfill our dreams. For example, I'd love to be back in college right now, but if I hadn't closed that door, I couldn't be helping people on a daily basis. There is a universal give and take, every day, all around us.

We are only here for a short time, and we need to make an effort to create a world that we are proud of. This next poem talks about the end of the world, because we *are* destroying the world as we know it. Toxic waste and chemical spills, scandal, abuse, global warming, fossil fuels, racism, hatred, gang warfare, terrorism, pharmaceutical blunders, poaching endangered species, the list goes on and on. If everyone simply looked inside themselves and tried to become the best humans they could possibly be, then all good things wouldn't end, they would simply change.

Our time here is miniscule compared to the legacy that we leave behind, whether good or bad, we all leave one, and this journey is only a fraction of the road we have in front of us. So, make your earth-walk count, because when it ends, it will be too late to begin.

God bless you, and thank you for allowing me to share my work with you.

THE END

Analyzing paradox
I slowly halt my gaze
Armageddon's coming
Shortly earth will feel the haze

Children crying, people dying
No one here conceives
The power of the Holy One
For no one still believes

The end of life is knocking
On the doorway to my soul
Evicting me of privacy
My spirit will unfold

Unraveling my precious thoughts
Unbinding bridled fears
Depriving me of sadness
For this end will dry my tears

Humanity will not escape
The danger we will find
The loss of our ambitions
Is the downfall of mankind

To alter this great tragedy
You need not ask me how
The problem of our great demise
Inside us, should stop now.

Lyrical Poet...

Throughout my years of writing poems, I almost always put them to music in my mind. The following are a series of songs I have written with the same thirst for expressing my thoughts in rhyming verse. I have written countless songs, but only included a few of my favorites in this compilation. Though they are difficult to read without the music that accompanies them, I felt they were important to share, because this entire collection represents who I am, as a poet, and as a man.

THE GOOD LIFE

Off the coast of Belize, I was watching as the waves
Tumbled on the beach
I was dreaming 'bout the stories, all the pirates and the glory
Of the treasures deep

But my gold's atop the water, with my wife, my sons and daughters
On a trusty craft
Where my heart recalls the faces of the times and all the places
Where I can't go back

Chorus:
I've got all that I want, I've got all that I need
So I won't go asking for more
Got a view of the swells, I got a boat and it sails
I've got a good life back on the shore

Repeat Chorus

Humid nights in Martinique, that can't be put to sleep
Dwell upon my mind-
The palm trees and the coconuts
Cocktails and the locals in the conga line

Live a peaceful life of ease, 'tween the mango trees
And the sun-filled days
'Cause the ocean is a potion, like a wave of locomotion
Catchin' all the rays

Chorus 2:
And I've got all the want, yeah I got all that I need
And I can't stop, 'til I get I get it right
I got a wonderful gig, a life I'm dyin' to live
And a girl that holds me tight!

Still I travel the globe to the places that are told of
On the TV screen
To the islands and the nations, to the dreams and fascinations
That calypso brings

So my band keeps playin' congas as I'm movin' to the sambas
In the songs we hear
Music soothin' while I'm groovin' like my body will be doin'
For a hundred years!

End Chorus:
And I've got all the want, I got all that I need
And I can't stop, 'til I get I get it right
I got a wonderful gig, a life I'm dyin' to live
And my girl she holds me tight!

I've got all that I want, I've got all that I need
So I won't go asking for more
Got a view of the swells, I got a boat and it sails
I've got a good life back on the shore

Got a view of the swells, I got a boat and it sails
I've got a good life back on the shore

A good life back on the shore...

YOU TOLD ME

You told me that you loved me,
And then you said goodbye-

You told me I was everything,
And our love would never die-

I shouldn't have believed in you,
'Cause now I'm stranded in the cold-

I shouldn't have believed the truth,
In every lie you told

Chorus 1
'Cause I need you
Like the morning needs the sun
Like a baby needs his mother
'Cause everybody needs someone
Oh I need you
If for one more night you'll hold me
Then I'll forget those promises
And I'll remember what you told me

I guess about a year has passed,
The way that time stands still-

It only seems like yesterday,
Our love was strong and real-

I wonder how you're makin' it baby-you were
Always proud and bold-

I wonder if you're thinkin' 'bout me baby,
And the things you never told–

Chorus 2
But I need you
Like the morning needs the sun
Like a baby needs his mother
'Cause everybody needs someone
Oh I need you
If for one more night you'll hold me
When you forget my promises
I'll remember what you told me

I shouldn't have believed you girl
Now I'm stranded in the cold

I shouldn't have believed the truth
In every lie you told

But I need you
Like the morning needs the sun
Like a baby needs his mother
'Cause everybody needs someone
Oh I need you
If for one more night you'll hold me
When you forget my promises
I'll remember what you told me

Then you'll forget my promises
And I'll remember what you told me....

OPEN

Waiting alone with your heart
Losing your mind to the game
Will you ever end what you start?
Hiding your world full of pain,

Maybe someday things will change
Hoping that time passes by
But all I can do here is wait
And all that my heart does is cry-

Chorus
Open up your eyes to me, and let your feelings go,
Ain't nothing in the world alive
That's gonna keep my lovin' home

So open up your heart to me
And let my lovin' in
I only wanna be with you
Don't you close me out again

Holding back more than your love
Knowing that this could be right
Looking for strength from above
While I lie awake in the night

Give me your heart and you'll find
A warmth you can feel nowhere else
A life without love is so blind
So don't close the door by yourself...

Chorus
Open up your eyes, and let your feelings go,
Ain't nothing in the world alive
That's gonna keep ambition home

So open up your heart to me
And let my lovin' in
I only wanna be with you
Don't close me out again

Open up your eyes to me, and let your feelings go,
Ain't nothing in the world alive
That's gonna keep ambition home

So open up your heart to me
And let my lovin' in
I only wanna be with you
Don't close me out again

Open up your eyes, and let your feelings go,
Ain't nothing in the world alive
That's gonna keep my lovin' home

Just open up your heart to me
And let my lovin' in
I only wanna be with you
Don't close me out again

Please don't close me out...a-gain...

A MYSTIC NIGHT

In a land far away where the sun never shines
The distance of space can get lost in the times

A lone band of soldiers create their own breed
And their inner beliefs form a strong sacred creed

An encompassing evil will always remain
And the long quest for freedom will drive you insane

Chorus:
Oh-oh there's no guiding light
On this mystic night
All hope is out of sight
But we won't give up the fight
Together we can find the light
In this mystic night
Oh-oh Cause it's a mystic.
It's a mystic Knight

With the hopes of a victory deep in their souls
The Knights will not halt to deliver their blows

The wounded and lifeless that scatter the ground
Will soon spread the word that there's light to be found

When the battles are over and peace has been one
The solemn young Knights, without fault will move on

Repeat Chorus

Glory will someday abolish the cries
And the world will expect not a greater demise

Till then there's a demon around every turn
And a savior within us that makes our hearts burn

So don't lift your focus from dreams in your sight
As you follow the steps of the brave Mystic Knight.

Repeat Chorus

THE GIRL

I found the girl-
And she's everything I need-
I found the girl-
And she can make a blind man see-

No one knows where she came from,
And no one knows her name-
No one knows what cross she bears-
But to me it's all the same...

Chorus
I found the girl, I found the girl
Hey-hey...I found the girl...

And I found the girl-
Who put the sunlight in my sky-
I found the girl-
Who put the future in her eyes-

I don't know how long she's been here,
I only hope she stays-
And I don't know how long it's been-
Since I have felt this way.... I found the girl...

(Repeat Chorus)

I found the girl-
With my dreams within her hands-
And I found the girl-
Who can make me understand-

Just how lonely life can be,
A game where no one wins-
A girl to spend her life with me-
To wash away my sins...

I found the girl...I found the girl...

RAISE YOUR HANDS

Many people in this world
Don't understand
A helping word
Means as much as a helping hand

And all the problems
In this world could disappear
If we could learn to love
We'd lose our fear

Chorus:
Raise your hands to the glory
Raise your hands to the love
Raise your hands to all mighty
Raise your hands up above

Every morning when I wake
He speaks to me
With the shining sun
And the birds up in the trees

A gentle smile
In the face of a stranger
And the stories He told
'Bout a boy in a manger-yeah

Repeat Chorus

I saw a small boy
Talking to a preacher man
He asked him "Mister,
Can you help me understand,

In a world of hatred, father
How can I do good
How will I know if I'm doing
All the things I should?"

Repeat Chorus

The preacher says
Raise your hands to the glory
Raise your hands to the love
Raise your hands to all mighty
Raise your hands up above

Many people in this world
Don't understand
A helping word
Means as much as a helping hand

And all the problems
In this world could disappear
If we could learn to love
We'd lose our fear

Repeat Chorus

In a world of hatred, father
How can I do good
How will I know if I'm doing
All the things I should

The Bible tells us
How to reach the Promised Land
For our time on earth
We've got to raise our hands!

Repeat Chorus

You've got to raise!!
Raise your hands to the glory
Raise your hands to the love
Raise your hands to all mighty
Raise your hands up above.

Anti-Rhyme...

By the time I was a freshman in college, I had already written countless poems, most of which I never saved and unfortunately will never be shared with the general public.

In my first year at the University of Kentucky, my love for poetry and an uncaring advisor suggested I take a graduate level poetry class, English 407.

This was the first and only poetry class I ever took because I believe true poets can be taught how to write, but not how to feel. Because my passion was couplet rhymes, and the teacher told me I wrote too much like a greeting card, the following poem is the first, and last non-rhyming assignment I ever completed in her class. The assignment; begin, and end your poem with the phrase, "Did I?"

Oh did I ever.

DID I?

Did I mention to you this morning
That my love flows for you
Like a river from the mountains?

Did I tell you that I fell in love with you
Like the raindrops fall from the sky?

Did I tell you that my love for you
Grows like the leaves grow on a tree
Deep within the forest

Did I hold you last night
The way you wanted me to hold you?

Did I express to you my feelings
When my heart cried out your name?

Did I tell you that my love has bloomed
Like the flowers in the field bloom each spring?

Did I say to you the sweet warm things
That you so deserve to hear?

Did I tell you that I loved you today?
Did I? Did I?

Thank you...

Special thanks to...

My parents for taking me around the world, and always reminding me that life is short and valuable, and you have to go for the gusto in everything that you do. I owe my adventurous nature to my mom, the scuba diving, paragliding nutcase that she is (she's also the smartest person I know, so I hope I got a couple of brain cells from her too). To my dad I owe my personality, my gab, my humor, my entrepreneurial spirit, and my love of sports and fun. He's truly one of a kind, and I am so lucky he's my dad. To both of them I owe my warm heart, they've always been such sweet people, not only to me, but also to everyone they meet. I couldn't have had two better role models growing up. I love you both so much, and thank you for all you've given me. You'll never know how much you are sincerely appreciated.

My sister Keri, for always being there, even when sibling rivalry got in the way. I could always turn to her, and she has supported me without fail, in everything I've ever done. From pizza, movies and pool time, to now, watching her family grow, she has always been a true friend, and an inspiration. My brother-in-law Matthew is an excellent father, husband and friend, and is helping raise their beautiful family; my loving nephew Connor, and his beautiful baby sister Katelyn. I love you all, what joy you've given us.

My grandmother Dorothy, hands down the most amazing 85 year old you'll ever be around, she is young at heart and I love her dearly. I believe she is actually more active than I am, over 50 years my senior. I love you grandma!

My amazing great-grandfather, Dr. Elwood Rowsey, he and his wife Grace actually raised my mother, when her parents were killed. Dr. Rowsey was an eloquent and skilled public speaker, a preacher, and a world-renowned debater. Listed in *Who's Who in America*, as the only man to ever defeat the infamous attorney Clarence Darrow in a debate, I can only hope that I got a little of his wisdom in my speech.

The entire McDaniel, Alexander and Rowsey clans, you have all meant so much to me, and I hope you know that.

The Tommy Burl, my best friend. Tozzy B. has been by my side through almost twenty years of friendship, nearly as long as I have been compiling these poems. He took me in when I was penniless, and he has supported my every move since we met in seventh grade. I thank you, and the entire Billings family for all of the love and support, especially these last years. You are my second family and I'm blessed to know you all.

The DLA, for your blue eyes, and curly golden locks. Your beautiful smile brings joy to the faces of everyone you meet, especially mine. My heart is alive with you in my life.

Dryboy Page, Jackie Jabberson Stall, and the PPP, without whom my Wednesdays and pizza cravings would never be the same. I have been friends with Ryan and Jason since first moving to Scottsdale in 1982. They have always helped me explore my artistic side, and have always been great friends to me. More importantly, they introduced me to Oingo Boingo, for which I am eternally grateful.

The UK Wildcats and the B-2 Bombers of Haggin Hall. You made five years of undergraduate go by in a flash, but left a lifetime of memories in your wake. I miss you.

The Marietta connection, and anyone who knows what the Big Chicken is. There are too many of you to name, but the rest of you know who you are (Jeffrey T., Travis and Michelle, Kyle and Kelly, Lumpy Steve, Gregory Scott, Seba Loco, Tiny Pork, the Brothers Evans, Tony Mack, the Reverend Z, the Woods, SuperNova, the nurse, my class officers, Serita C., Dicky V, and the Flying Wallenda. Our time together in Georgia is priceless.

My employers and co-workers from beginning to end, every job was important and helped make me who I am today. The McFletcher Corp, Scottsdale TPC, Mammoth Cave National Park, Wyncom, Inc., Lakeside Golf, Wood Family Chiropractic, Life University Student Clinic, Chiropractic Family Care, and especially FNF Construction (F.O.T.Y. 2002). I appreciate every life lesson I gained by working for you, and with you.

The Masonic brethren at Scottsdale 43, that are behind me every step of the way, I appreciate your warmth, acceptance, and brotherhood. I hope we always meet upon the level; I truly value the friendships I've made. Eric will always be first base to me.

Scottsdale First Christian church, my first church home, such fond memories.

The soundtrack of my life: the music and lifestyle of Jimmy Buffett has reinforced the desire in me to rhyme, dive, sail, surf and live each day to the fullest. I also feel that Bob Marley, reggae in general, Oingo Boingo and especially Danny Elfman had immeasurable influence in the rhymes that I share with you.

My love for television and movies continuously inspires me. I often consider myself a mixture of a goofy Hawkeye Pierce and a determined Thomas Magnum, because I can go from one to the other in a heartbeat. From *Superman* and *Peter Pan* to *Indiana Jones* and *The Goonies*, my ageless youth will follow me always, and I pray that never changes. Hopefully Club 33 will see to that.

My current patients that have helped me establish myself in private practice (God knows I am no good unless I'm my own boss). I have been blessed with a patient base that trusts me, and that I consider to be my friends. From the people that pop in every once in a while, to the "*favorite* patients" and "Susan T's" of the world that make it all worthwhile. I'm blessed by your Chiropractic compliance in an otherwise *medical* world. I'm truly grateful for my profession, as it has afforded me the ability to help more people than I could have ever possibly imagined.

The Great Architect of the universe, I know you have a plan for my life. I love what you've done with it so far and I can't wait to see what you've got in store for my future!

To anyone that I failed to mention, if you have ever held a special place in my heart, I hope you know who you are, and I thank you, sincerely.

CMM

The End.

978-0-595-39854-6
0-595-39854-5

Printed in the United States
58426LVS00004B/323